Yorkshire Dales &
Youth Hosteller's Wal...

by

Martyn Hanks

Stenkrith Falls

Martyn Hanks is a professional model maker living near Preston. His work has taken him from London to Australia, Saudi Arabia and the Caribbean. A strong desire to travel has led him to visit over 100 countries, youth hostelling in many of them.

Martyn is a member of the YHA Northern Region Council. These walking maps resulted from a wish "to give something back" to the YHA. Encouraged by YHA staff, he has now mapped most of the youth hostels in the north of England. His book of walking maps, **The Lake District: Youth Hosteller's Walking Guide**, was published by Landmark Publishing in June 1997.

Martyn has also held several exhibitions of his paintings including exhibits at the Harris Art Gallery, Preston and at the University of Central Lancashire.

Booking Bureau

yha

A Service for Independent Walkers.

Herriot Way ❖ *Coast-to Coast*
Pennine Way ❖ *Cumbria Way*
White Peak Way

*The easy and convenient way to plan your walk. Let us book your accommodation for you along the route. You tell us the dates and your itinerary - we do the rest. **All ages welcome!!***

♦ *Youth Hostels, some guesthouses and camping barns*
♦ *Dinner, bed & breakfast & packed lunches available. Plus self-catering facilities. You choose to meet your budget.*
♦ *Comfortable bunk-bedded rooms, lounges, drying facilities for wet clothing and boots.*
♦ *Low administration costs. Just 50p per person per night to organise your holiday.*

***YHA - Welcoming walkers
for over 60 years***

***Send a large s.a.e. to:
YHA, P.O.Box 11, Matlock,
Derbyshire   DE4 2XA
stating which walk(s) you are
interested in.***

Yorkshire Dales & Moors

Youth Hosteller's Walking Guide

by

Martyn Hanks

The hamlet of Bordley

Published by:
Landmark Publishing Ltd,
Waterloo House,
12 Compton,
Ashbourne,
Derbyshire   DE6 1DA   England

ISBN 1 901522 41 5

British Library Cataloguing in Publication Data:
A catalogue record for this book is available from the British Library

Printed in Italy

Designed by Carreg Ltd, Ross-on Wye, Herefordshire
Cover design: Mark Titterton & Sam Witham

Acknowledgements

The publishers wish to thank the following for their assistance: Colin Logan, YHA Chief
Executive, Liz Lloyd, YHA Business Development Director, Gill Chapman, and Barbara
Southam at YHA Northern Regional Office.
The text was written principally by Lindsey Porter, with the assistance on the route
descriptions by Martyn Hanks and Brian Witty.

Safety Note:

**The majority of the walks in this book are low level. It is strongly recommended that
the OS map be carried on all high level walks, which should be avoided in bad
weather.**

Foreward by Colin Logan, Chief Executive
of the Youth Hostel Association of England and Wales

I am sure that many readers of this invaluable and interesting guide book will need no reminding of the importance of Youth Hostels to our National Parks and other wonderful stretches of countryside. Indeed many of you will be taking advantage of the YHA's network of accommodation in the Yorkshire Dales and Moors as you read it.

Others of you may feel that you are too mature or too fond of your creature comforts to darken the doors of a Youth Hostel. Or perhaps you have only partly happy memories of school trips of many years ago and a recollection of a spartan regime in which it was mainly the shared discomfort which engendered camaraderie!

The YHA continues to serve the needs of hundreds of thousands of walkers, cyclists, schoolchildren, families, foreign backpackers and myriad other travellers every year. The accommodation remains simple and affordable by all but it is also comfortable, welcoming and well maintained. In an area such as the Yorkshire Dales we offer a unique and incomparable range of experiences in terms of the location and setting of our properties.

As our President, David Bellamy, wrote last year "While others have recently discovered the concept of sustainable tourism, our aim from the start has been to instill knowledge and love for the countryside, and an understanding of the deeper values associated with our environment and heritage".

Much of the time you may be more concerned with the tiredness in your legs or the shortness of your breath. But when you pause to take in the fantastic landscape views which the walks described in this book offer you, I am sure that you will think of these deeper values - as indeed you will when you arrive at a Youth Hostel after your strenuous day out and enjoy the warmth of hospitality and companionship to be found there.

I hope that you enjoy this guide and find the walks from it to be rewarding.

CDC Logan

Walks around Youth Hostels

Inter-Hostel Walking Routes

The Youth Hostels

Hostel

Aysgarth (1)
Beverley (2)
Boggle Hole (3)
Earby (5)
Dentdale (4)
Ellingstring (6)
Grinton Lodge (7)
Hawes (8)
Haworth (9)
Helmsley (10)
Ingleton (11)
Keld (12)
Kettlewell (13)

Kitby Stephen (14)
Linton (15)
Lockton (16)
Malham (17)
Mankinholes (18)
Osmotherley (19)
Scarborough (20)
Slaidburn (21)
Stainforth (22)
Thixendale (23)
Wheeldale (24)
Whitby (25)

Hotel descriptions are given alphabetically from page 195 onwards

Figures in brackets refer to the numbers on the area map on page 8/9

About This Book

Yorkshire is fortunate in having two National Parks. However they differ considerably in character. The Dales is a limestone region known for its beauty, both in the dales or valleys and in the character of its villages. The North York Moors is essentially a gritstone moorland. It is picturesque nonetheless, especially in the autumn when much of the moor is cloaked in the purple flowers of the heather.

This book consists of walks around the youth hostels in these two areas plus several inter-hostel walking routes. Also included are Thixendale and Beverley Friary which are south of the North York Moors, and a group of hostels in the Pennines just outside Yorkshire - Kirkby Stephen, Dentdale, Ingleton and Slaidburn.

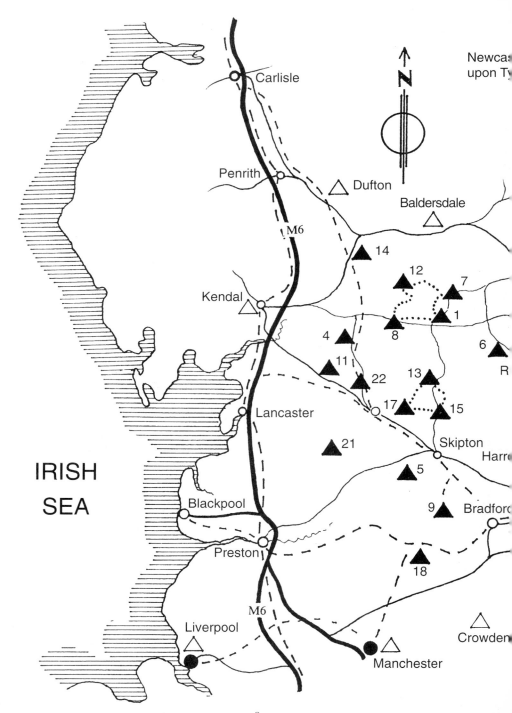

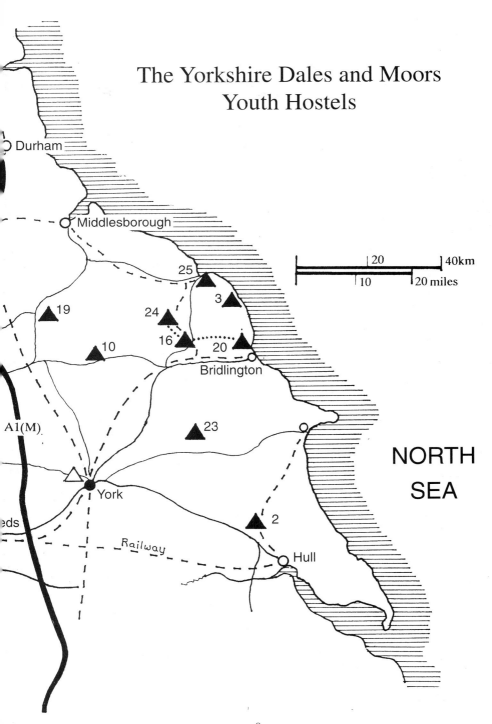

The Yorkshire Dales and Moors
Youth Hostels

"What is the YHA?"

"To help all, especially young people of limited means, to a greater love and care of the countryside, particularly by providing hostels or other simple accommodation for them in their travels, and thus to promote their health, rest and education". These aims, set out when the Youth Hostels Association first began in 1930, remain as important as ever. The Association grew from the dedicated effort of visionary people and provided a firm foundation for recent years which has seen great strides in upgrading and the development of new hostels.

Images are often outdated - of spartan surroundings, rules and regulations and a belief that hostels are only for young people. Today, a Youth Hostel signifies good value accommodation which is friendly, comfortable, dependable and secure, backed up by an assurance of standards which apply to Youth Hostels around the world.

The 237 Youth Hostels throughout England and Wales provide a major national resource. Together, they account for over 14,000 bedspaces which places the YHA in the top league of accommodation providers. But it is the location of the hostels which makes them a truly unique asset. Over the years, sites have been found in some of our most spectacular landscapes, in remote hill country, on Heritage coasts, or lowland woodland settings. Many Youth Hostels are in villages or small towns, where they are close to the countryside but also are accessible to other facilities and form part of the local community. The hostels in the Yorkshire Dales and Moors range in size and comfort from former shooting lodges to pretty village cottages and Victorian mansions: many are in incomparable locations ideal for walkers.

As a body of some 270,000 members in England and Wales, the YHA is a social movement, enabling people of all ages to meet others in a special atmosphere of friendship. The international movement, of which YHA England and Wales forms a part, is rightly seen as a force for peace and understanding. Membership of YHA England and Wales entitles people to travel and hostel in over 60 countries around the world with more than 5,000 Youth Hostels to choose from.

Whilst others have recently discovered the concept of "sustainable tourism", the aim of the YHA from the start has been to instill a knowledge and love of the countryside and an understanding of the deeper values associated with our environment and heritage. This has always come first; our accommodation is a means to an end. Increasingly, there is a wide range of types of hostel, clearly indicated so that members can select which one is likely to meet their particular needs. Yet throughout, our firm principle is that the simple, recognisable character of Youth Hostels is always retained.

From its inception, the YHA has been an environmental movement which has worked with its own resources to implement sustainable tourism principles in practice. We have a seven point Environmental Charter for Youth Hostels worldwide which underlines our commitment to important issues such as reducing consumption, recycling and conserving energy.

The Youth Hostels in Yorkshire exemplify the YHA with their wide range of opportunities to explore all parts from the bustling market towns and Dales villages to the remote and little visited moors. The YHA is a member organisation and you will be asked to show your membership card on arrival at a Youth Hostel. If you are not already a member, you can join at the first Youth Hostel you visit or alternatively contact YHA for a membership form (you will find a special voucher entitling you to a free one year's membership on the last page of the Lake District book in this series). You will receive a free annual guide listing all the hostels in England and Wales and receive a regular members' magazine and discounts on travel, places of interest and shops.

Booking your stay is easy - simply telephone or write to the hostel of your choice. Alternatively, you can book a bed ahead from most hostels.

When you stay at a Youth Hostel you will sleep in comfortable bunk bedded rooms sharing with people of the same sex, unless you have made special arrangements in advance - for instance, families or groups of friends may be able to aquire rooms with fewer beds, often with their own washing facilities. Otherwise, you will find showers, toilets and washing facilities close to your room. You will be given freshly laundered bed linen with which to make up your bed. Pillows, duvets and/or blankets are also provided.

At most Youth Hostels you will find comfortable sitting areas for relaxing and socialising, as well as facilities such as drying rooms, cycle stores and local information. While many hostels have areas specially set aside for smoking, there are also many "No Smoking" hostels. At small Youth Hostels - to keep prices low - you may be asked to help with simple household tasks. You are asked to clear up after yourself.

Circular routes from hostels are popular with walkers who like to spend several nights in one place, exploring the countryside from their base. If you are a member of a walking club or simply a group of friends and family you can choose in the winter to rent a whole Youth Hostel for your group under the YHA's 'Rent a Hostel' scheme. Some of the smaller Youth Hostels in Yorkshire are available - with a key for you to come and go as you please and good self-catering facilities for all your meals. A brochure on 'Rent a Hostel' explains how to book and is available by 'phoning 01727 855215.

YHA has been spending considerable sums of money refurbishing its buildings and improving standards of comfort and privacy. Each year, more hostels are identified for improvement, a few more properties open for business for the first time, and those surplus to requirements are closed.

Today YHA is a vibrant organisation catering for the needs of young and old. So long as you are young at heart, a warm welcome awaits you!

Liz Lloyd
Business Development Director

Walks Around The Hostels

Aysgarth Youth Hostel (OS Outdoor Leisure Map 30)

Map 1 (see page 14/15)

Aysgarth to Castle Bolton   8 miles (12.5km)

From the Youth Hostel cross the River Ure to Freeholders Wood where the former railway line is met. The path climbs uphill and away from the river with a lane to Carperby on your right. After four fields, the path crosses the lane to reach the village. Turn right, and then left after passing the pub. The path climbs up onto the moor before turning east and dropping slowly down into Castle Bolton. It is a picturesque village with a fourteenth century castle. There is a W.C. here near to the church, which is opposite the castle.

Continue through the village before turning right at the end of the main street. The path crosses the field before reaching the Carperby Road, on the outskirts of Redmires village. Leave the lane at Low Bolton along Thoresby Lane. The latter eventually continues as a path, keeping High Thoresby Farm to your right, turning south to reach Hollinshouse Farm and the River Ure again. Ahead is Freeholders Wood where you can take time out to enjoy Aysgarth Falls.

Map 2 (see page 16/17)

Aysgarth to West Burton   5.5 miles (8.7km)

Come out of the Hostel and turn left on the A684, turning right over the stile opposite the vicarage. The path climbs over a small hill before dropping down to the Bishops Dale at Eshington Bridge. Cross the latter and turn right through the river meadows before turning to your left to reach West Burton on the B6160. This is crossed and a little lane brings you into the main street. Upon reaching The Green, turn left and walk to the Walden Beck where there is a footbridge. Look for Cauldron Falls which is slightly upstream. Upon crossing the bridge the path climbs uphill to reach an old lane, known as Morpeth Gate, which should then be followed past Morpeth Scar where there are several view points. The lane is fairly flat as it heads eastwards, where it is known as High Lane. After passing an old quarry, a track to the left leads down to a wood and the remains of a preceptory of the Knights Templars. Beyond this it is a short distance to reach the B6160 opposite a folly tower. Turn left on the main road and, after, crossing the Walden Beck again (at Hestholme Bridge), a path to the right crosses to the fields heading for Aysgarth Church, which is just below the Youth Hostel.

Notice on the map the short cut which can be taken from West Burton. It crosses the fields keeping Ellers Lane (B6160) to your left meeting the latter just before Hestholme Bridge.

Aysgarth to Eshington Bridge   2.5 miles (4km)

Take the route as above to Eshington Bridge. A path then proceeds down the side of the Bishopdale Beck, past a caravan site, to reach the A8684 near to Hestholme Bridge. Walk down to the bend in the road by the bridge and then turn left, crossing the fields close to the River Ure. There are two paths which head for the church. The one closest to the river is recommended so that you can see the waterfalls.

Map 3 (see page 18/19)

Aysgarth to Askrigg   10.5 miles (16.7km)

This route goes up the River Ure to Askrigg. The path keeps close to the river for much of the way. Skeldale House in Askrigg has become particularly well known as the fictional vet's surgery in James Herriott's **All Creatures Great and Small**. Return through Newbiggin and Carperby, where James Herriott spent his honeymoon. On the way to Carperby the route passes Disher Force, a small waterfall.

Several stiles on this path are, for ease, marked by yellow painted dots. They are shown on the map.

Beverley Youth Hostel

Map 4 (see page 20/21)

Beverley to Tickton and Arram   8.5 miles (13.5km)

Upon leaving the youth hostel, turn left and right to reach the A1079. The route follows the road and then the Beverley Beck to its confluence with the River Hull. This is then followed through Tickton village towards Arram; where one leaves the river to return via the perimeter of a MOD airfield. There is a bridge over the Beverley bypass, returning to the youth hostel along Woodhall Way.

The map also highlights a short 4 miles (6.5km) town trail which goes to Black Mill.

Map 5 (see page 22/23)

Beverley to Skidby Windmill   11 miles(17km)

From nearby Beverley Minster, the route picks its way through fields and past three farms and a golf course to reach the magnificent windmill at Skidby. The fully restored mill, built in 1821, is open most weekends and some week days, Tel 01482 884971. A return route via Beverley Black Mill is shown, otherwise telephone 01482 884057 to enquire about bus times.

Map 1
Walks around Aysgarth YH:
Aysgarth to Castle Bolton
see page 12

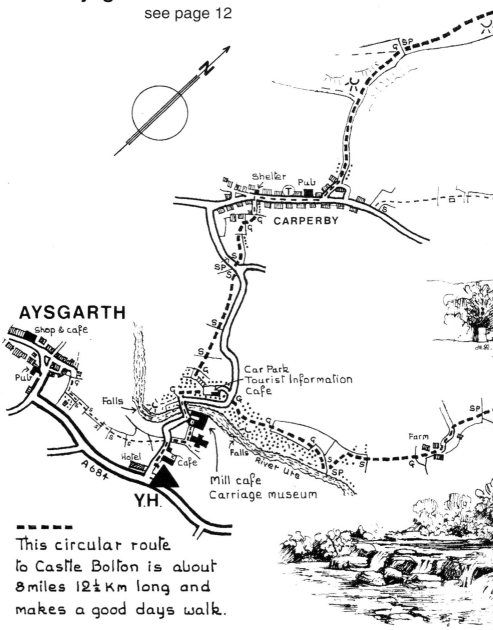

N

Shelter Pub

CARPERBY

SP

AYSGARTH

Shop & cafe

Pub

Falls

Car Park
Tourist Information
Cafe

Falls River Ure

Farm

SP

Hotel Cafe

Mill cafe
Carriage museum

A684

Y.H.

This circular route
to Castle Bolton is about
8 miles 12½ Km long and
makes a good days walk.

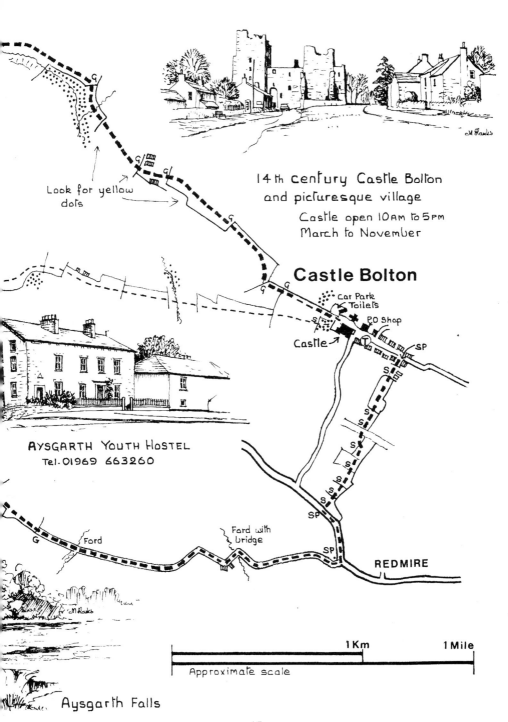

Look for yellow dots

14th century Castle Bolton
and picturesque village

Castle open 10am to 5pm
March to November

Castle Bolton

Car Park
Toilets

P.O. Shop

Castle

SP

AYSGARTH YOUTH HOSTEL
Tel. 01969 663260

Ford

Ford with bridge

REDMIRE

Aysgarth Falls

| | 1 Km | 1 Mile |
Approximate scale

15

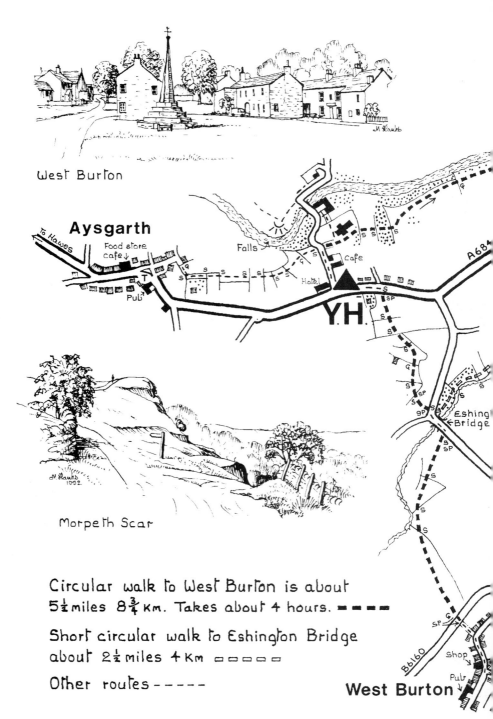

West Burton

Aysgarth

To Hawes

Food store
cafe

Falls

Cafe

Hotel

A684

T

Pub

Y.H.

Eshing
Bridge

Morpeth Scar

Circular walk to West Burton is about
5½ miles 8¾ km. Takes about 4 hours. ■ ■ ■

Short circular walk to Eshington Bridge
about 2½ miles 4 km □ □ □ □ □

Other routes - - - - -

B6160

Shop

Pub

West Burton

Map 2
Walks around Aysgarth YH:
Aysgarth to West Burton
see page 12

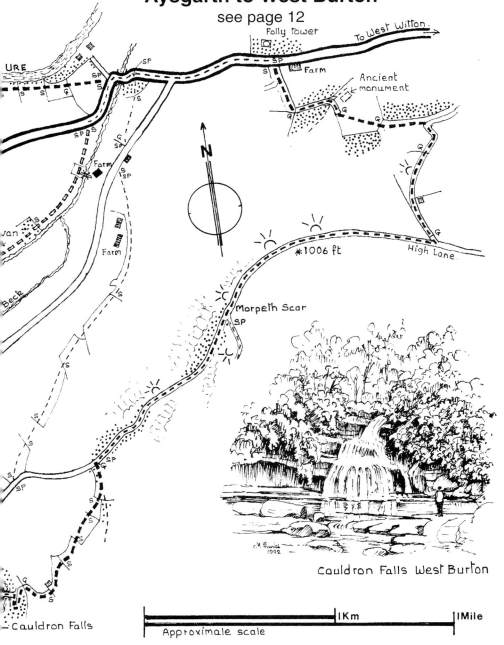

Cauldron Falls West Burton

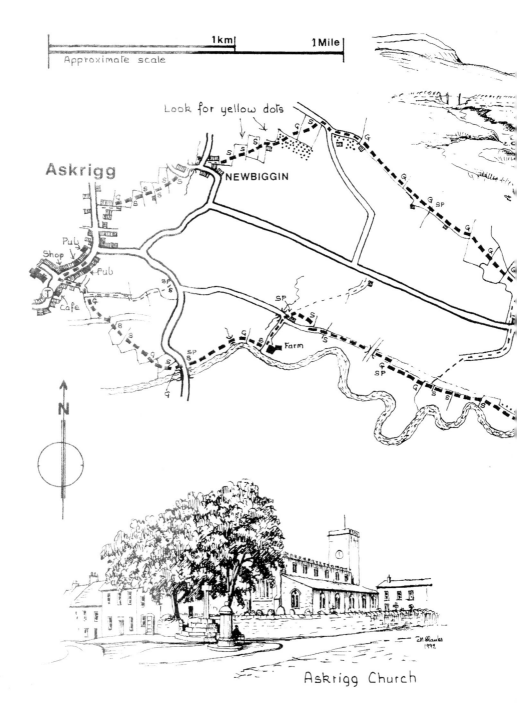

Approximate scale

1 km 1 Mile

Look for yellow dots

Askrigg

NEWBIGGIN

Pub
Shop
Pub
Cafe
Farm

N

Askrigg Church

18

Map 3
Walks around Aysgarth YH:
Aysgarth to Askrigg
see page 13

This circular day walk is around
10½ miles 16¾ km long ▬▬▬

Other routes ─ ─ ─ ─ ─

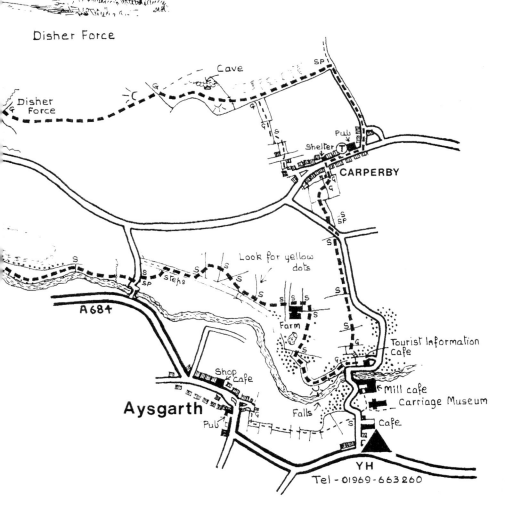

Disher Force

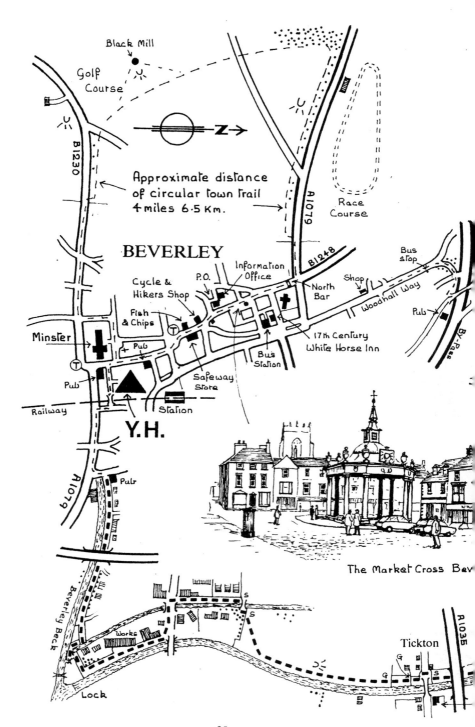

Black Mill

Golf Course

Z →

Approximate distance
of circular town trail
4 miles 6·5 Km.

Race Course

B1230

A1079

B1248

BEVERLEY

Information Office

P.O.

Cycle & Hikers Shop

North Bar

Shop

Bus stop

Woodhall Way

Pub

By-Pass

Fish & Chips

Minster →

Pub

Pub

17th Century White Horse Inn

Bus Station

Safeway Store

Pub

Railway

Station

Y.H.

A1079

Pub

The Market Cross Bev

Beverley Beck

Works

S

S

Tickton

A1035

Lock

G

G

S

Map 4
Walks around Beverley YH:
Beverley to Tickton and Arram

see page 13

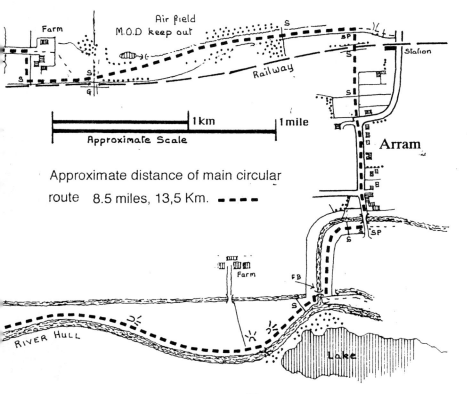

Beverley Friary Youth Hostel Tel: 01482-881751

Farm

Air field
M.O.D keep out

Railway

Station

1 km   1 mile

Approximate Scale

Approximate distance of main circular
route   8.5 miles, 13,5 Km. ▬ ▬ ▬

Arram

Farm

FB

RIVER HULL

Lake

Map 5 Walks around Beverley YH:
Beverley to Skidby Windmill

see page 13

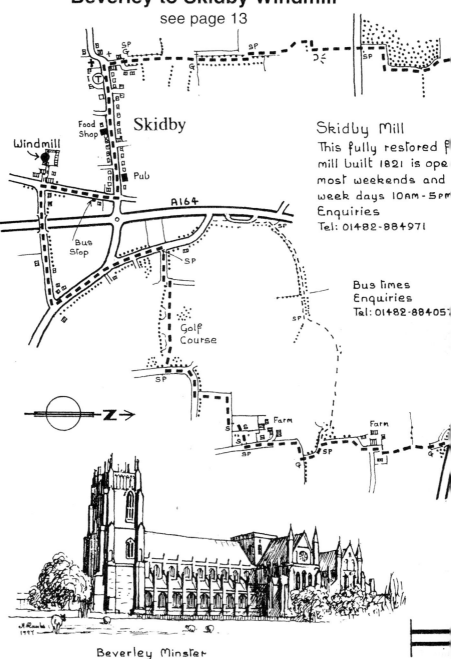

Skidby

Windmill

Food Shop

Pub

A164

Bus Stop

Golf Course

Skidby Mill
This fully restored f
mill built 1821 is ope
most weekends and
week days 10AM-5PM
Enquiries
Tel: 01482-884971

Bus times
Enquiries
Tel: 01482-88405

Farm

Farm

Beverley Minster

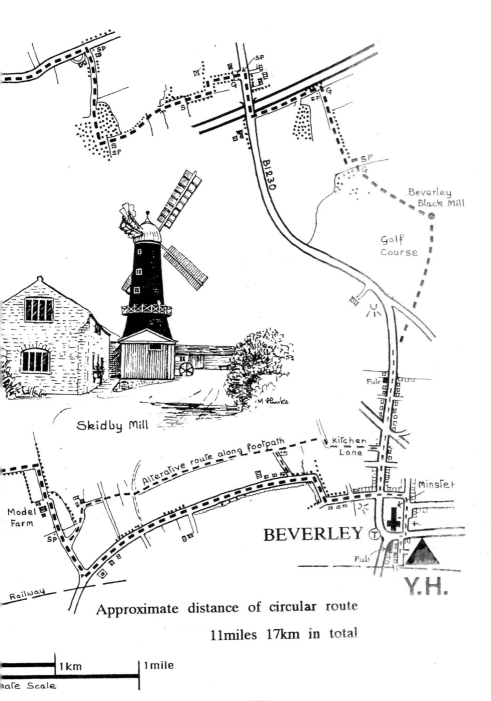

Skidby Mill

Beverley
Black Mill

Golf
Course

Alterative route along footpath

Kitchen
Lane

Model
Farm

Minster

BEVERLEY

Pub

Railway

Y.H.

Approximate distance of circular route

11miles 17km in total

1km   1mile

ate Scale

23

Boggle Hole Youth Hostel

Map 6 (see page 26/27)

Boggle Hole to Ravenscar   6 miles (9.5km)

From the hostel walk up the road away from the coast before turning left to cross the fields to reach a disused railway line close to Browside Trekking Centre. Go through the bridge and then join the line, following it for 2 miles (3km) to reach Ravenscar where there is a National Trust Coastal Centre, cafe and toilets.

The return route heads for the coast which is followed back to the youth hostel. The position of the cliff path is subject to change owing to erosion of the cliff.

For a shorter path, note the route shown from near Browside Trekking Centre which heads to the coast. This makes a userful evening stroll.

Map 7 (see page 28/29)

Boggle Hole to Fyling Hall and Robin Hood's Bay   6 miles (9.5km)

This route may have to be done in reverse if you wish to walk along the beach between the hostel and Robin Hood's Bay. There is a cliff path if you have to avoid the beach.

The path heads inland initially before heading back to the sea past Fyling Hall School. It is wooded in places. After passing the school, the path heads for Fylingthorpe before reaching Robin Hood's Bay. The old port of the village is very picturesque. It's only a short walk from here to the youth hostel, either on the sand or above the cliffs. Note the postion of bus stops for Whitby and Scarborough, if needed.

Dentdale Youth Hostel (OS Outdoor Leisure Map 2)

Map 8 (see page 30/31)

Dentdale to Dent Village   12 miles (19km)

Leave the Youth Hostel and turn left, following the River Dee on the Dales Way. The path crosses the river and, having reached the local pub and a further three fields, your route bears to the left. The path climbs a little and offers an alternative to walking along the road, reaching the River Dee at Ewedales Bridge. Turn left and, after passing two fields, the Dales Way bears off to the left, passing through a wood and several fields before dropping down to the River Dee. The Dales Way crosses the river and proceeds along a well defined path to Dent Village. On route, the path leaves the River Dee and crosses the fields to reach The Deepdale Beck at Bridge End.

As a diversion, you can join the road here and walk back to visit the National Park, Cave and Fell Centre at Whernside Manor. From Dent Village, cross the river and return on the path which runs back down the valley above the minor road. It eventually joins the road with a 3 mile walk back down the latter to the Youth Hostel. Alternatively, cross the lane and the River Dee to reach the Dales Way, and retrace your steps back to the Youth Hostel.

Map 9 (see page 32/33)

Dentdale to Ribblehead Viaduct   10 miles (16km)

This walk should only be made in good weather, unless you are well equipped.

    Leave the Hostel and walk down the road and underneath the railway line. Follow the road up past the wood on your right on the Dales Way. The latter climbs up past the wood and then bears south-east along the track known as Black Rake Road. The initial part of this section may be boggy in places. The path keeps above Highgayle Farm before descending to meet the B6255, the Blea Moor Road. Turn right upon reaching the road heading towards Ribble Head. For much of the way there is a path at the side of the road. Opposite the B6479 to Settle, the path turns to the right with the Ribblehead Viaduct directly in front of you. The path keeps to the right of the railway track and then follows a route directly above the railway which enters a tunnel a mile or so from the Viaduct. You will pass three air shafts before the railway reappears and the path heads for Dent Head Farm, passing a small waterfall on route. After passing the farm the path crosses the Fell End Gill where you turn left for the Youth Hostel.

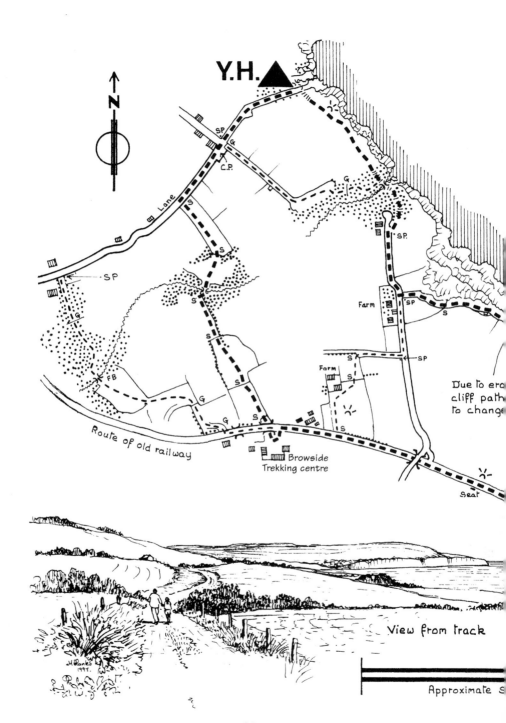

Y.H.

N

Lane

SP
G
C.P.
S
S
S
S
S
S
G
G
FB
G
G
Route of old railway
Browside
Trekking centre

SP
SP
Farm
S.P.
Farm
S
S
SP
S
S
S

Due to ero
cliff path
to change

Seat

View from track

Approximate S

26

Map 6
Walks around Boggle Hole YH:
Boggle Hole to Ravenscar
see page 24

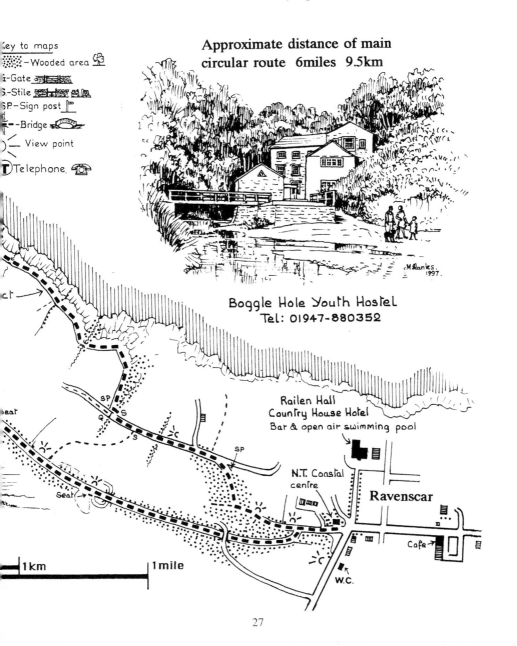

Key to maps
- ::::: –Wooded area
- G-Gate
- S-Stile
- SP–Sign post
- <--Bridge
- View point
- T Telephone.

Approximate distance of main circular route 6miles 9.5km

M.Danks. 1997.

Boggle Hole Youth Hostel
Tel: 01947-880352

Railen Hall
Country House Hotel
Bar & open air swimming pool

N.T. Coastal centre

Ravenscar

Cafe

W.C.

1km   1mile

Map 7 Walks around Boggle Hole YH:
Boggle Hole to Fyling Hall and Robin Hood's Bay
see page 24

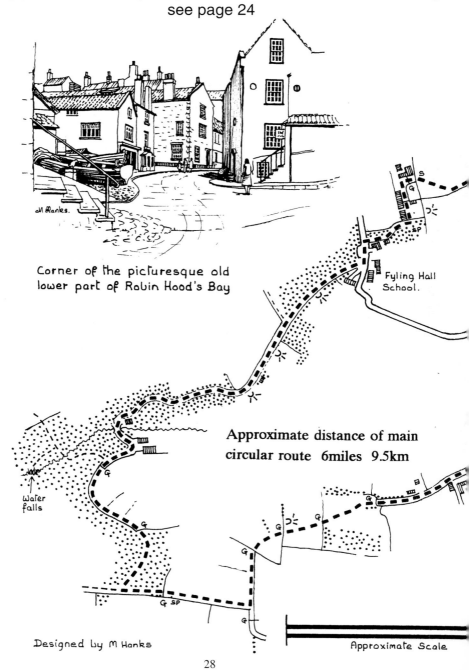

Corner of the picturesque old
lower part of Robin Hood's Bay

Fyling Hall
School.

Approximate distance of main
circular route 6miles 9.5km

Water
falls

Designed by M Hanks

Approximate Scale

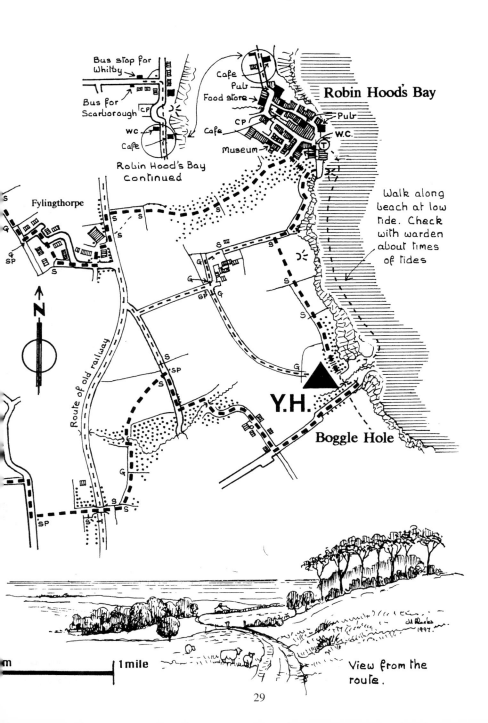

Bus stop for Whitby

Bus for Scarborough

WC

Cafe

Cafe
Pub
Food store →

Robin Hood's Bay

CP

Pub

W.C.

Cafe

Museum →

Robin Hood's Bay
Continued

Fylingthorpe

Walk along beach at low tide. Check with warden about times of tides

N

Route of old railway

Y.H.

Boggle Hole

1 mile

View from the route.

29

Map 8
Walks around Dentdale YH:
Dentdale to Dent Village
see page 24

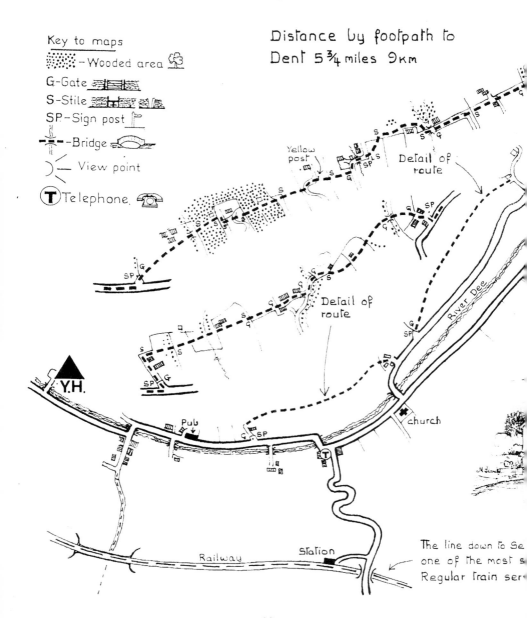

Key to maps

- Wooded area

G–Gate

S–Stile

SP.–Sign post

– Bridge

)— View point

(T) Telephone.

Distance by footpath to
Dent 5¾ miles 9km

Yellow post

Detail of route

Detail of route

River Dee

Y.H.

Pub

church

T

Station

Railway

The line down to Se
one of the most s
Regular train ser

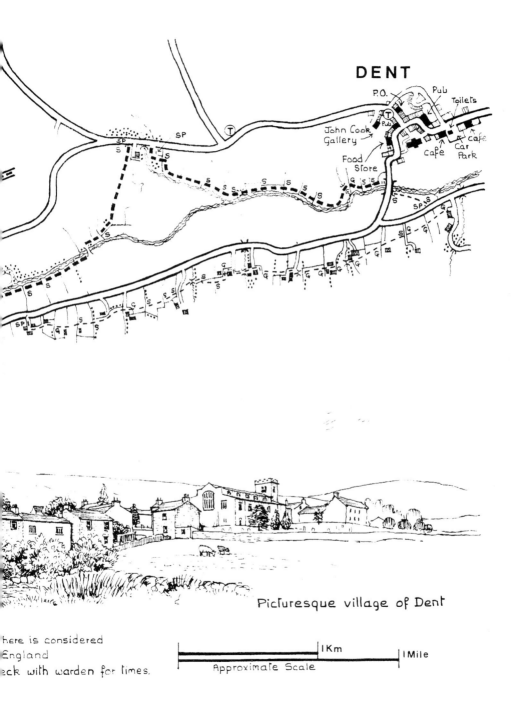

DENT

P.O.
Pub
Toilets
John Cook
Gallery
Pub
SP
SP
S
T
Food
Store
Café
Café
Car
Park
G
S
S
S
S
S
S
S
S
S
S
SP
G
G
G
S
S
S
G
G
S
G
G
S
S
G
G
S
S
S
S
S
SP
G
S

Picturesque village of Dent

here is considered
England
eck with warden for times.

|1Km
|1Mile
Approximate Scale

31

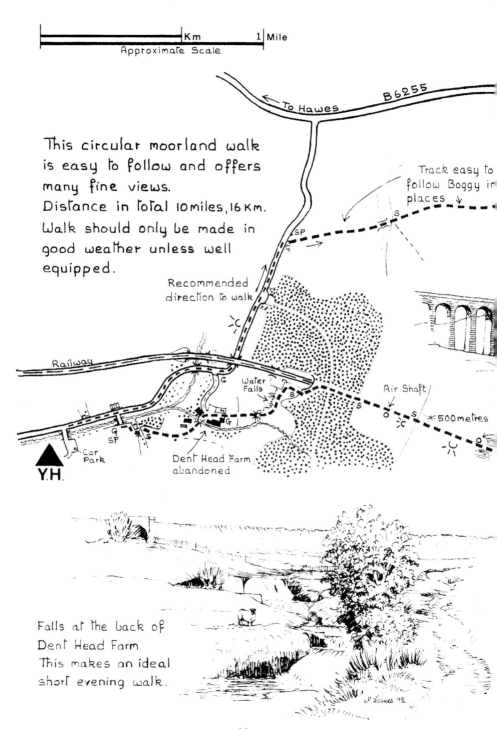

Approximate Scale

Km   1 | Mile

← To Hawes   B6255

This circular moorland walk is easy to follow and offers many fine views.
Distance in total 10 miles, 16 Km.
Walk should only be made in good weather unless well equipped.

Track easy to follow Boggy in places

Recommended direction to walk

Railway

Water Falls

Air Shaft

500 metres

Car Park

Y.H.

Dent Head Farm abandoned

Falls at the back of Dent Head Farm
This makes an ideal short evening walk.

32

Map 9
Walks around Dentdale YH:
Dentdale to Ribblehead Viaduct
see page 25

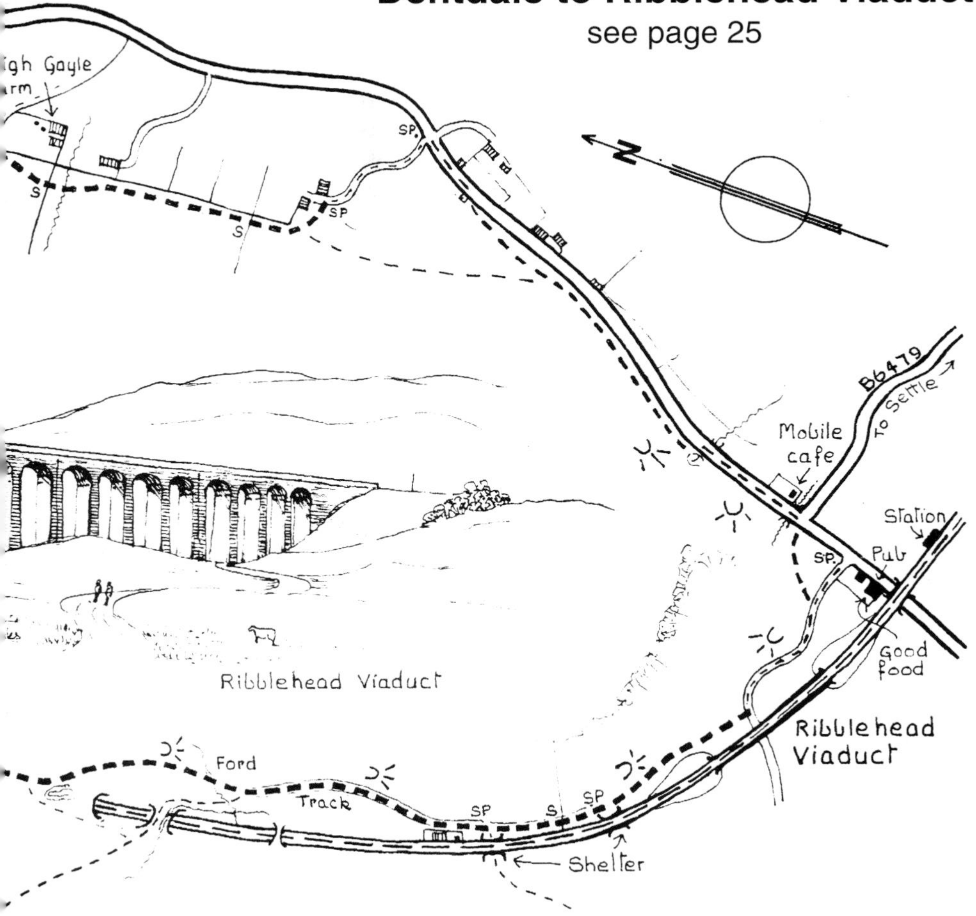

High Gayle Farm

SP

S

SP

S

N

B6479

To Settle

Mobile cafe

Station

Pub

SP

Good Food

Ribblehead Viaduct

Ribblehead Viaduct

Ford

Track

SP

S

SP

Shelter

Dentdale Youth Hostel Tel 015396-25251

Earby Youth Hostel

Map 10 (see page 36/37)

Earby to Barnoldswick and Thornton-in-Craven   7 miles (11.2km)

From the Youth Hostel go down into Earby, pass under the old railway line heading westwards through the fields to Barnoldswick which is only a couple of miles away.Upon reaching a river turn right and follow this until it reaches the B6252 where the canal is reached. Follow the canal tow-path for a mile and a half and then turn right, leaving the canal behind and heading for Thornton-in-Craven. Cross the B6252 and proceed straight ahead over the old railway line and through a farm, before turning right to cross the fields for the final half mile or so to the Youth Hostel.

Map 11 (see page 38/39)

Earby to Lothersdale   7.5 miles (12km)

Take the track at the back of the hostel which passes a farm for the open moorland. Head for a gate in the wall and turn right in a south-easterly direction. The path crosses a road on a short section of the Pennine Way before bearing off to the right across a couple of fields to reach a lane which takes you into Lothersdale. The woollen mill here still has its waterwheel, although it no longer powers the machinery. To the east of the village is Stone Gappe, used by Charlotte Brontë as Gateshead Hall in *Jane Eyre*. To return to the Youth Hostel, take the road to Raygill before cutting across the fields back to Earby. Look out for the small waterfall just before the Youth Hostel is reached.

In Earby you may visit the seventeenth century grammar school which is now a lead mining museum.

Ellingstring Youth Hostel

Map 12 (see page 40/41)

Ellingstring to Masham   9 miles (14.5km)

Leave the hostel, turning left and then right and right again to join a path which runs across the fields to High Ellington. The path proceeds through the village and across the A6108 heading for High Mains Farm. Here the path does a 'U' turn to follow the River Ure to reach Masham where the A6108 crosses the river. At Masham there are pubs and a café plus a fish and chip shop. The village is famous for the Theakston Brewery which has a visitor centre. Tours are available from noon until 4.00pm. There is also a glass-making centre off the main square. The return path starts from near to the brewery and crosses through fields to reach Fearby. The route follows a lane from Fearby to Ellingstring.

Ellingstring to Jervaulx Abbey   3.5 miles (5.5km)

This is a short walk from the far end of the village from the Youth Hostel. It heads north through five fields to reach the A6108. This is crossed and ahead is Jervaulx Park with the Abbey ruins. There is a cafe which is reached by turning left upon reaching the A6108. The return route cuts through the park and runs more directly back to the Youth Hostel. Note that there is a longer route, returning via High Ellington and part of the outward route to Masham, but this involves some walking alongside of the A6108. The abbey was built by Cistercian monks in the twelfth century and the remains are substantial.

Map 10
Walks around Earby YH:
Earby to Barnoldswick and
Thornton-in-Craven

see page 34

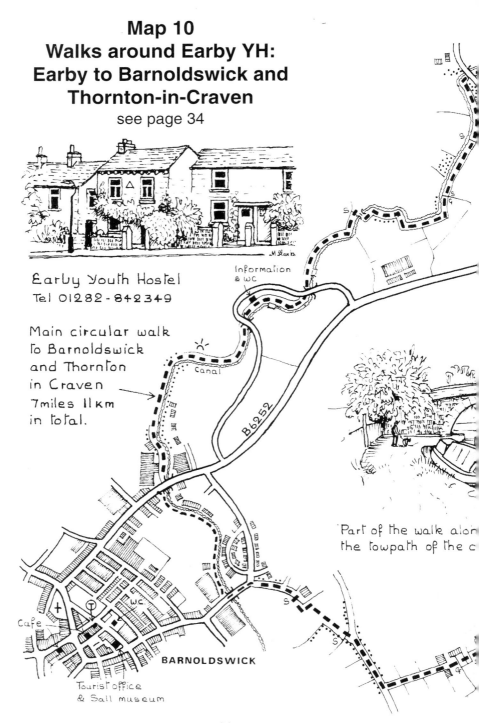

Earby Youth Hostel
Tel 01282-842349

Main circular walk
to Barnoldswick
and Thornton
in Craven
7miles 11km
in total.

Information & WC

Canal

B6252

Part of the walk along
the towpath of the c

Cafe

WC

BARNOLDSWICK

Tourist office
& Sail museum

M. Banks

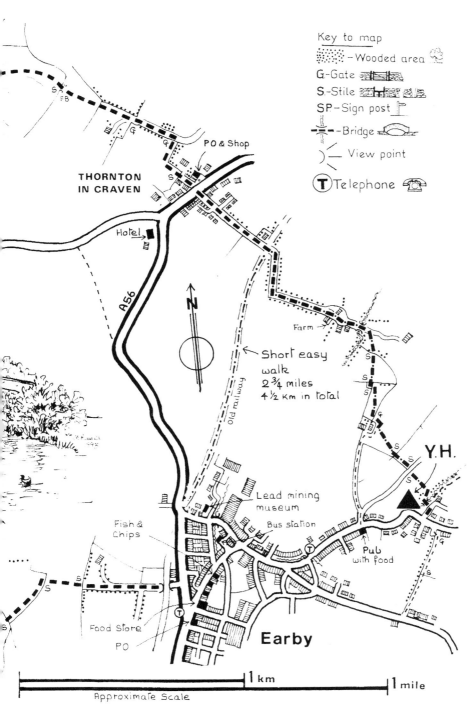

Key to map

:::::: – Wooded area

G – Gate

S – Stile

SP – Sign post

– Bridge

) – View point

(T) Telephone

THORNTON IN CRAVEN

PO & Shop

Hotel

A56

N

Short easy walk 2¾ miles 4½ Km in total

Old railway

Farm

S

S

S

G

S

S

Y.H.

S

Lead mining museum

Bus station

Pub with food

Fish & Chips

Food Store

PO

T

T

Earby

S

S

|⎯⎯⎯⎯⎯⎯⎯⎯⎯⎯⎯⎯⎯⎯⎯⎯⎯| 1 km | 1 mile

Approximate Scale

37

Map 11
Walks around Earby YH:
Earby to Lothersdale

see page 34

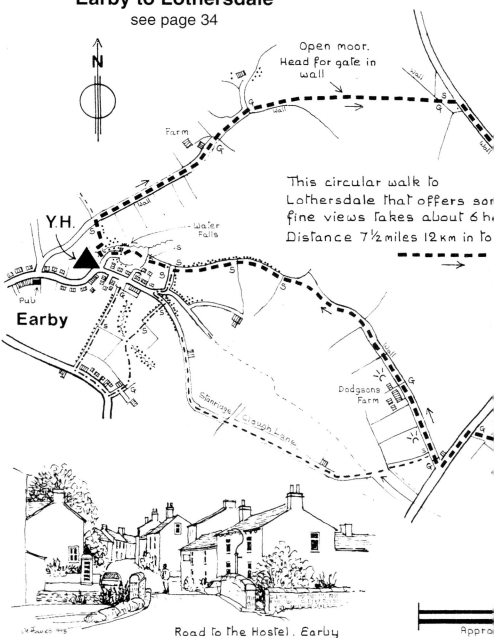

N

Open moor.
Head for gate in
wall

Wall

Wall

S

G

Wall

Farm

G

Wall

Y.H.

S

Water
Falls

S

S

S

S

S

This circular walk to
Lothersdale that offers som
fine views takes about 6 h
Distance 7½ miles 12 km in to

Pub

Earby

S

S

G

G

Wall

Dodgsons
Farm

G

G

Stanriage

Clough Lane

G

Road to the Hostel. Earby

Appro

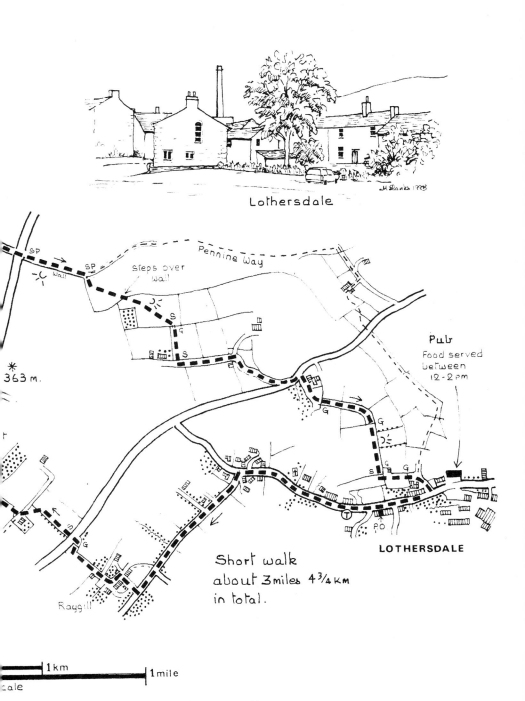

Lothersdale

M.Banks 1993

Pennine Way

SP

SP

Wall

Steps over
Wall

S

G

S

G

S

363 m.

Pub

Food served
between
12-2 pm

G

G

G

G

S

S

G

T

P.O.

LOTHERSDALE

Short walk
about 3 miles 4¾ km
in total.

S

G

Raygill

1 km

1 mile

Scale

Abbey

Jervaulx Park

Cafe & Car.P.

SP

Farm

A6108

Jervaulx Abbe

Farm

Green

Warden

Ellingstring

Y.H.

High Ellington

Circula 9 miles

Circula 3 ½ mi

Farm

St Marys church Masham

1km 1mile

Approximate Scale

40

Map 12
Walks around Ellingstring YH:
Ellingstring to Masham and
Jervaulx Abbey
see page 35

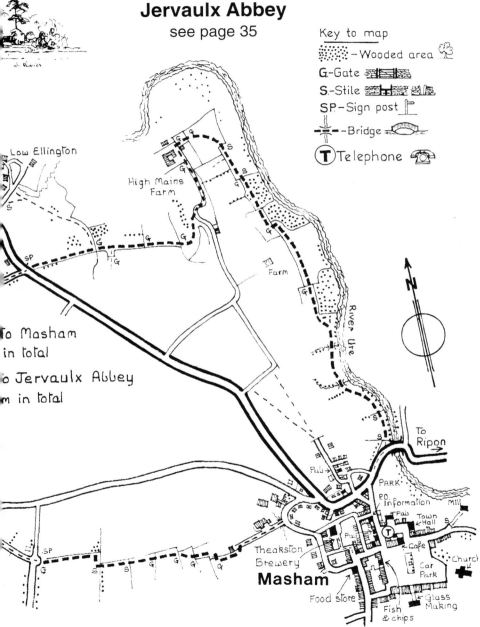

Key to map
- Wooded area
- G-Gate
- S-Stile
- SP-Sign post
- Bridge
- (T) Telephone

Low Ellington

High Mains Farm

Farm

Farm

River Ure

N

To Masham
in total

To Jervaulx Abbey
m in total

To Ripon

PARK

P.O.
Information

Mill

Pub

Pub

Town Hall

Theakston Brewery

Café

Car Park

Church

Masham

Food store

Fish & chips

Glass Making

SP

G

S

S

G

G

G

G

41

Grinton Lodge Youth Hostel (OS Outdoor Leisure Map 30)

Map 13 (see page 44/45)

Short evening stroll   2.7 miles (4.5km)

For an easy evening walk, take the path from the back of the Hostel which follows the stream down to Cogden Hall. Upon reaching a minor road, turn right and then right again to cross through five fields to reach the Grinton-Leyburn road. The road is crossed to inspect an old smelting mill, before turning north to re-join the road and return down it to the Hostel.

Grinton to Reeth   5 miles (8km)

Turn right at the front of the hostel and left at the 'T' junction before bearing right and taking a gap through the heather. This path cuts across several of fields to reach the River Swale where a footpath enables you to continue on and into Reeth. Proceeding through the village on the Grinton Road, you cross the Arkle Beck and turn right by a signpost through a gate to cross through three fields to reach Grinton by the roadbridge over the River Swale. You can either return down the main road, or turn left by the pub and then right by a signpost to cross through four fields on a path running in the general direction of the Youth Hostel.

Map 14 (see page 46/47)

Grinton to Langthwaite   10.7 miles (17km)

This walk includes part of Fremington Edge. It offers fine views but should only be used in good weather.

Proceed into Grinton and, at the bridge over the River Swale, turn left onto the path to Reeth. From Reeth the path goes up the Arkle Beck before turning right to climb steeply up Cuckoo Hill onto Fremington Edge. After about a mile the path descends down into the valley, passing Fell End lead mine and then Storthwaite Hall to reach the village of Booze and then Langthwaite. Perhaps regrettably, the pub is in Langthwaite rather than Booze! The return path follows the Arkle Beck passed Storthwaite Hall before crossing a footbridge and returning through the fields to Reeth. From here you can either head straight back to Grinton or follow in reverse the Reeth/Grinton path referred to above.

There are numerous shafts on Fremington Edge and the Marrick Moor. These should be avoided.

LANDMARK VISITORS GUIDE:
YORK AND YORKSHIRE DALES

By Ron Scholes

* **Full colour touring guide**

* **Approximately 240 pages**

* **The author has spent a lifetime exploring and photographing the area**

* **Included in the text are**
- history and geography of the area
- walks and other outdoor activities
- places to visit
- houses, gardens and architecture
- cycle and scenic motor routes
- literary and artistic connections
- festivals and public entertainments

* **AND a detailed Landmark FactFile including accommodation, restaurants, public transport etc.**

Send for details to:

LANDMARK
Publishing Ltd ● ● ●

Waterloo House, 12 Compton, Ashbourne, Derbyshire DE6 1DA England

Key to map

- ▨ – Wooded area 🌳
- G – Gate
- S – Stile
- SP – Sign post
- ✛ – Bridge
- ⌒ View point
- ⋀ Cairn
- Ⓣ Telephone

To Keld ←

B6270

Pub
Bakery
W.C.
Swaledale Museum
Cafe
Pub
Bank
P.O.
Cafe
Tourist Office
Reeth
Food Store

River Swale

FB SP

G

N

Reeth

Easy e
circula
2 ¾ mile
i

1 km
Approximate Scale
1 miles

44

Map 13
Walks around Grinton Lodge YH:
Grinton to Reeth
see page 42

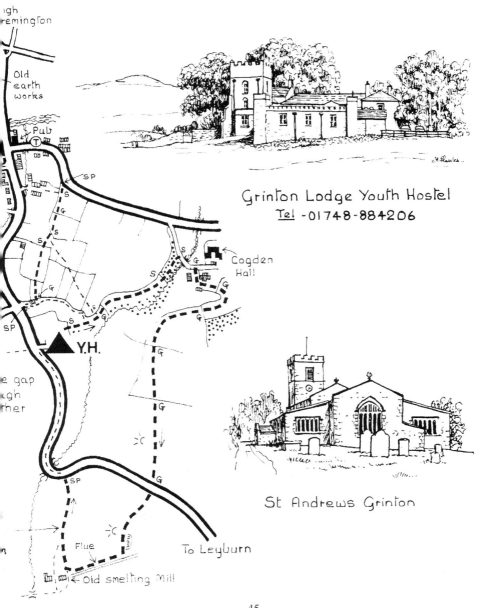

Grinton Lodge Youth Hostel
Tel -01748-884206

St Andrews Grinton

k
aite

igh
remington

Old
earth
works

Pub
T

SP
S

G

S
S

G

SP

Y.H.

e gap
igh
her

Cogden
Hall

S
G

S

G

G

G

SP
G

C

Flue

C

Old smelting Mill

To Leyburn

45

Booze

Langthwaite

1 km   1 mile

Approximate Scale

Map 14
Walks around Grinton Lodge YH:
Grinton to Langthwaite

see page 42

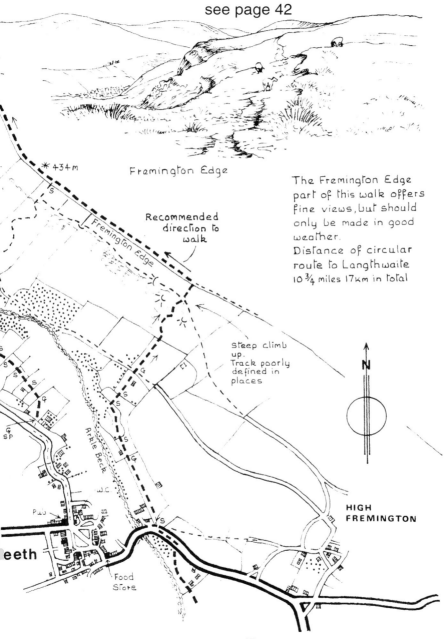

* 434 m

Fremington Edge

Recommended
direction to
walk

Fremington Edge

The Fremington Edge
part of this walk offers
fine views, but should
only be made in good
weather.
Distance of circular
route to Langthwaite
10 ¾ miles 17km in total

steep climb
up.
Track poorly
defined in
places

N

HIGH
FREMINGTON

Arkle Beck

W.C

P.15

eeth

Food
Store

SP

Hawes Youth Hostel (OS Outdoor Leisure Maps 2 and 30)

Map 15 (see page 50/51)

Hawes to Cotterdale   9.5 miles (15km)

From the Hawes to Appersett Road the path crosses the fields to reach the old railway line at Appersett Viaduct which spans the Widdale Beck. A lane follows the Beck into Appersett where the river is bridged. The path then follows the A684 down to the River Ure for about two miles to reach Mossdale Head Farm. Upon joining the road, turn right and cross the river (the Mossdale Gill). The path then crosses the A684 and the River Ure before climbing uphill to reach Cotterdale. The route back cuts through the fields (eventually becoming poorly defined) to reach the Pennine Way. Just follow the contour around, and the latter will be intersected. Turn right and then follow the Pennine Way down into Hard Raw where you can visit Hardraw Force (waterfall). Continue across the fields to reach the Brunt Acres Road which runs back into Hawes.

Hawes to High Clint   7.7 miles (12.5km)

This is a walk which should not be done in bad weather. Take the lane off the A684 in the centre of Hawes to Sedbusk. It crosses the River Ure at Haylands Bridge, then a path to the right cuts across the fields to Sedbusk. It goes over an old pack horse bridge soon after leaving the road. These had no or just low side walls which did not interfere with the panniers on the sides of the horses.

From Sedbusk, which has a pony trekking centre, take the unmade Shutt Lane and then a path which leads up onto Abbotside Common between High Clint and Smuker Hill. The track is poorly defined at one point, as it ascends between the two hills, but look for marker posts with yellow painted tops.

The path then follows fairly flattish ground past High Clint and Pike Hill to reach a lane which descends down to Simonstone, where a path connects with Hardraw. It is worth inspecting Hardraw Force; the entrance is through the Green Dragon Inn at Hardraw (see map). The waterfall is said to be the highest single drop waterfall in England. From here a path leads to Burnt Acres road which is reached near to Haylands Bridge.

Map 16 (see page 52/53)

Hawes to Aysgill Waterfall   3.5 miles (5.6 km)

This short walk, ideal for an evening stroll, proceeds from Hawes to nearby Gayle. Follow the Duerley Beck up into Sleddale, past Gayle Force, a waterfall upstream of the bridge in Gayle. The path runs along the river bank past Aysgill Force (which is about 30 feet high). This is an attractive walk with a long series of minor waterfalls. Return along an old gated lane back to Gayle.

Hawes to Burtersett   3.5 miles (5.6 km)

Another short walk leaves Gayle on a path which crosses the fields to the south east of
Hawes to join Shaws Lane, which runs into Burtersett. It returns directly to Hawes,
joining the A684 on the outskirts of the village. An alternative path branches off and heads
directly to Gayle. It joins a minor road and passes an old earthwork on your left just
outside the village.

There is a National Park Centre and the Upperdales Folk Museum in Hawes village.

Haworth Youth Hostel

Map 17 (see page 54/55)

Haworth to Brontë Bridge   10.2 miles (16.5km)

Proceed down into the charming 'old world' atmosphere of Haworth village and to the
railway station. This is one of several on the Keighley and Worth Valley Railway, which
has featured in *The Railway Children* by E Nesbit. It is a preserved line, run by enthusi-
asts, with steam-hauled services.

A path runs down the valley to Oxenhope, keeping close to the railway. Here, you
pass Oxenhope Station before climbing away towards Brontë Bridge. The route is a
mixture of footpaths and quiet lanes, eventually reaching the picturesque clapper bridge.
From here, the path reaches a lane which runs into Stanbury. Proceeding through the
village, a path turns to the left and drops down into the Worth Valley, heading for
Oakworth, which is close to the Youth Hostel.

Map 18 (see page 56/57)

Haworth to Oakworth   2 miles (3km)

This short walk goes down to the preserved Haworth Station and proceeds up the river
valley to Oakworth, returning down lanes and the hill back up to the hostel. It can be
extended by exploring the cobbled streets of gritstone houses in Haworth and the Brontë
Museum at the Parsonage, near to the Church.

There is a Museum of Childhood in Haworth and, of course, the railway can be used
to take you to Oakworth and Oxenhope Stations, returning on foot.

Cotterdale

Ford

SP

Cotterdale

G

G

Steps
in wall

SP

Pennine W

G

Track poorly defined
follow contour round

LS

LS

LS

LS

SP

A684

Farm

SP

G

Turners
seat

Farm

S

G

Mossdale Head
Farm

Old railway viaduct.
Waterfalls.

1 km   1 mile

Approximate scale

50

Map 15 Walks around Hawes YH:
Hawes to Cotterdale and High Clint

see page 48

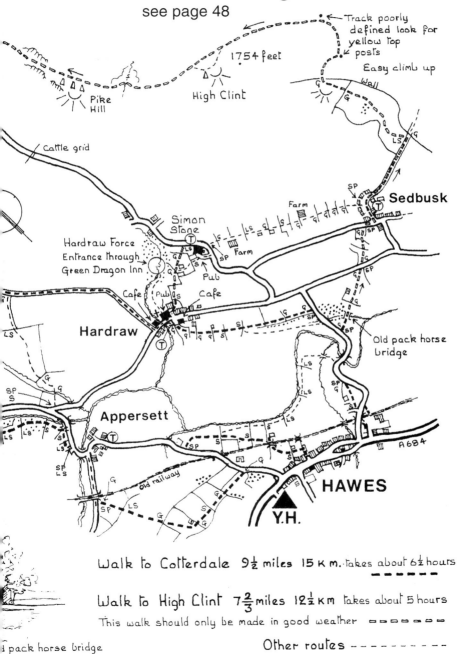

Track poorly defined look for yellow top posts

Easy climb up

Well

1754 feet

High Clint

Pike Hill

Cattle grid

LS

SP

Farm

Sedbusk

Simon Stone

Hardraw Force Entrance through Green Dragon Inn

Farm

Pub

SP

Cafe

Pub

Cafe

Hardraw

LS

Old pack horse bridge

SP S

LS

Appersett

A 684

Old railway

HAWES

Y.H.

Walk to Cotterdale 9½ miles 15 K m. takes about 6½ hours

Walk to High Clint 7⅔ miles 12¼ km takes about 5 hours

This walk should only be made in good weather

pack horse bridge   Other routes

51

Map 16
Walks around Hawes YH:
Hawes to Aysgill Waterfall
and Burtersett

see page 48

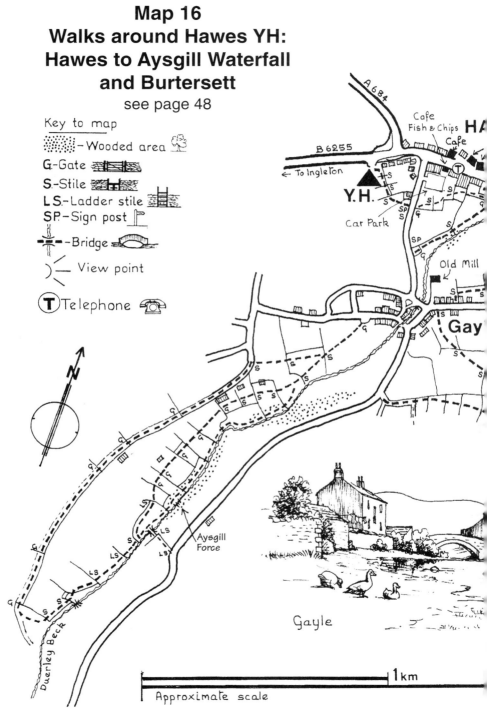

Key to map

- ░░░ – Wooded area
- G.-Gate
- S.-Stile
- LS.-Ladder stile
- SP.-Sign post
- ▬▬ -Bridge
-)⟨ – View point
- (T) Telephone

N

A 684

Cafe
Fish & Chips HA
Cafe

B 6255

← To Ingleton

Y.H.

Car Park

Old Mill

Gay

SP

Aysgill
Force

LS
LS
LS
LS

Gayle

Duerley Beck

1 km

Approximate scale

52

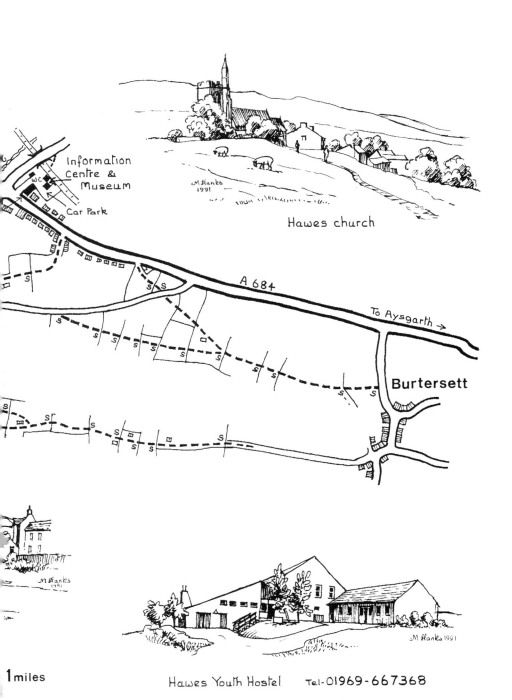

Information
Centre &
Museum

W.C.

Car Park

Hawes church

M Hanks
1991

A 684

To Aysgarth →

Burtersett

M Hanks
1991

1 miles

Hawes Youth Hostel   Tel· 01969 · 667368

53

Map 17   Walks around Haworth YH:
Haworth to Brontë Bridge
see page 49

M. Planks 1993

Brontë Bridge

Farm

SP

To Colne

Bus Stop

Pub

PO

SP

SP

STANBURY

(T)

Reservoir

SP

Distance of circular walk to Brontë
10 ¼ miles 16 ½ km in total. ----→

S

G

LS

SP

SP

LS

SP

Café

Brontë Bridge

Water Falls

SP

* 315 m

SP

G

G

Farm

Reservoir

| | 1 km | | 1 mile |

Approximate Scale

54

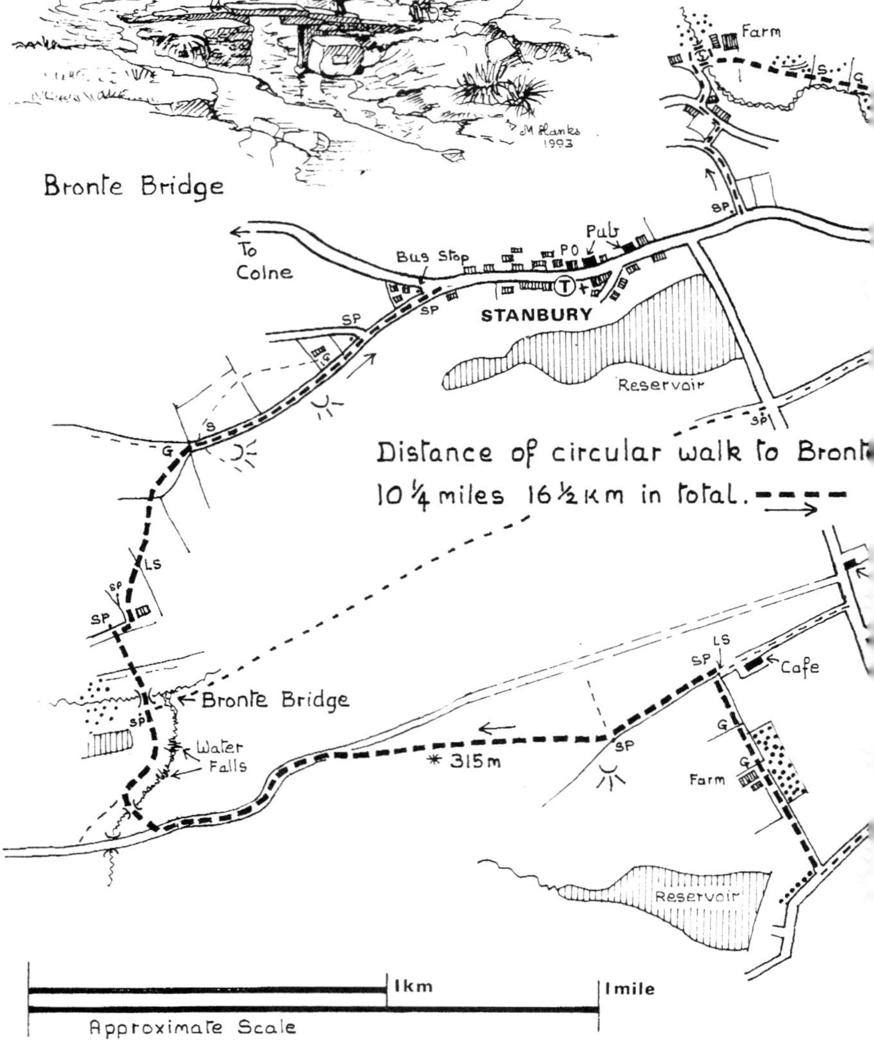

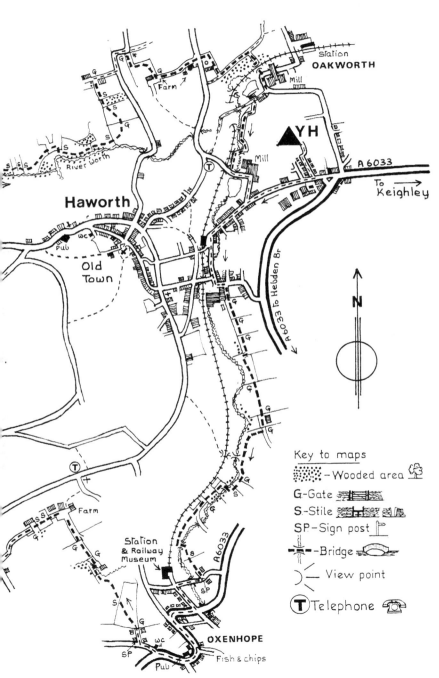

Station
OAKWORTH
Farm
Mill

YH
Mill
A 6033
To Keighley

River Worth

Haworth

Pub
wc
Old
Town

A 6033 to Hebden Br.

N

Farm

Station
& Railway
Museum
A 6033

S
SP

OXENHOPE
Fish & chips
wc
SP
Pub

Key to maps
⬡ - Wooded area
G - Gate
S - Stile
SP - Sign post
- Bridge
View point
T Telephone

55

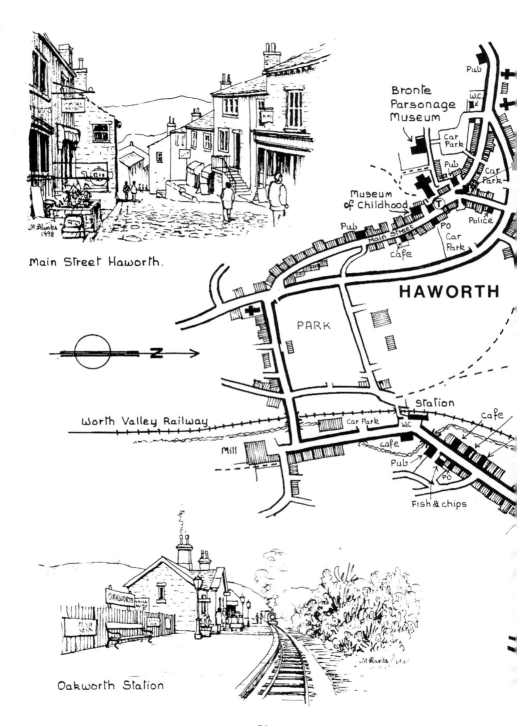

Main Street Haworth.

Bronte Parsonage Museum

Pub

W.C

Car Park

Pub

Car Park

Museum of Childhood

Pub

Main Street

PO Car Park

cafe

Police

HAWORTH

PARK

N

Worth Valley Railway

Station

cafe

Car Park

W.C

Mill

cafe

Pub

PO

Fish & chips

Oakworth Station

OAKWORTH

Map 18
Walks around Haworth YH:
Haworth to Oakworth

see page 49

see page 49

Haworth Youth Hostel Tel-01535-642234

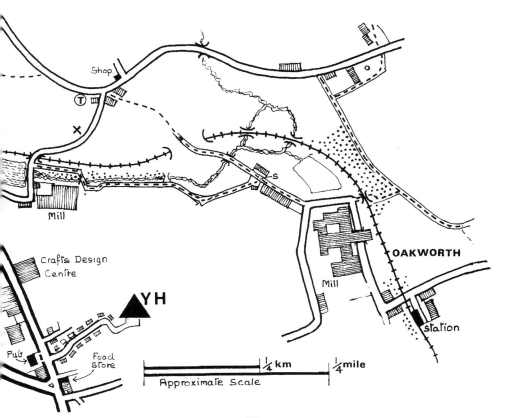

st Information
ntre

ll
om

Shop

T

Mill

Crafts Design
Centre

YH

Pub

Food
Store

Mill

OAKWORTH

station

¼ km   ¼ mile

Approximate Scale

Helmsley Youth Hostel

Map 19 (see page 60/61)

Helmsley to Rievaulx   9.5 miles (15km)

Leave Helmsley from near the castle, past the car park. There is a good view of the castle with its unique D-shaped keep. The path goes through the park to Duncombe House, until recently used as a girls' school but now once more occupied by the owners as a residence. There is a charge for entrance to the park. This was originally laid out with a driveway to Rievaulx Terrace, with its two temples overlooking Rievaulx Abbey. Part of this is used as your path.

Upon reaching a minor road, turn left and then right by the River Rye to visit the impressive remains of Rievaulx Abbey, now owned by English Heritage. Before leaving here, proceed past the church up the hill to Rievaulx Terrace, now owned by the National Trust. Emerging from a wood you arrive at a huge terrace with a temple at each end. There are exhibitions in these worth seeing, and the terrace makes a lovely picnic spot overlooking the abbey.

From the abbey, return by taking a path upstream, before crossing a bridge and returning to the minor road met previously. There are good views across the meadows to the abbey ruins. Return through the park. The map shows an alternative route to reach Duncombe House. Note that refreshments are available here, but not at Rievaulx.

Note the short evening walk marked on this map.

Map 20 (see page 62/63)

Helmsley to Rye Farm   4.5 miles (7km)

This relatively short walk follows the River Rye down to a fish farm at Rye Farm. The river is crossed here; go through the fields to near Low Woods Farm, returning down the farm drive to Helmsley.

Helmsley to Pockley   4.5 miles (7km)

This alternative short walk crosses fields to join a track in a wood, which is followed before a footbridge enables you to join a farm track to Pockley, where one returns to Helmsley.

Both of these short walks take about two hours.

Map 21 (see page 64/65)

Helmsley to Harome and Nunnington   12 miles (19km)

Although a long walk, it is on the flat and enables you to visit the lovely Nunnington Hall (check opening times) where the cafe obligingly opens at 1.30pm.

Follow the River Rye before crossing under the former railway bridge to reach the Helmsley to Harome road. Once in the village, a path returns to the river and follows it down to Nunnington. The seventeenth century hall houses the Carlisle collection of miniatures. Return through the fields to Harome, from where you can retrace your steps to Helmsley along the River Rye or take the more direct road.

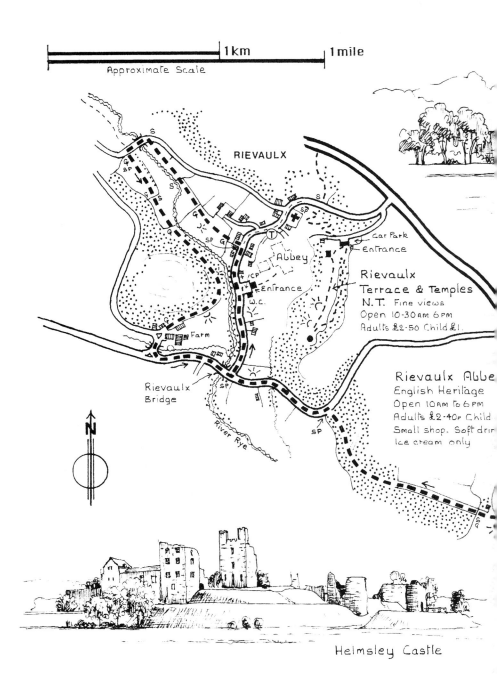

1km   1mile

Approximate Scale

RIEVAULX

Car Park
Entrance

Abbey

Rievaulx
Terrace & Temples
N.T. Fine views
Open 10·30AM 6PM
Adults £2·50 Child £1.

Entrance

W.C.

Farm

Rievaulx
Bridge

Rievaulx Abbe
English Heritage
Open 10AM To 6PM
Adults £2·40P Child
Small shop. Soft drin
Ice cream only

River Rye

N

Helmsley Castle

60

Map 19   Walks around Helmsley YH:
Helmsley to Rievaulx   see page 58

Rievaulx Abbey

M.Slater 1995

Duncombe House

Short evening walk

Childrens play area

B1257

F.B.

Y.H.

Car Park

steeps

Refreshments

Duncombe Park

Castle

Temple

Duncombe House

Entrance to Park £1

Helmsley

P.O.

River Rye

good weather ick

This is a full days walk, about 9½ miles 15km. Please note there is no cafe or pub at Rievaulx.

Map 20
Walks around Helmsley YH:
Helmsley to Rye Farm and Pockley
see page 59

Two easy 4 ½ mile 7 km circular walks
Both take about 2 hours

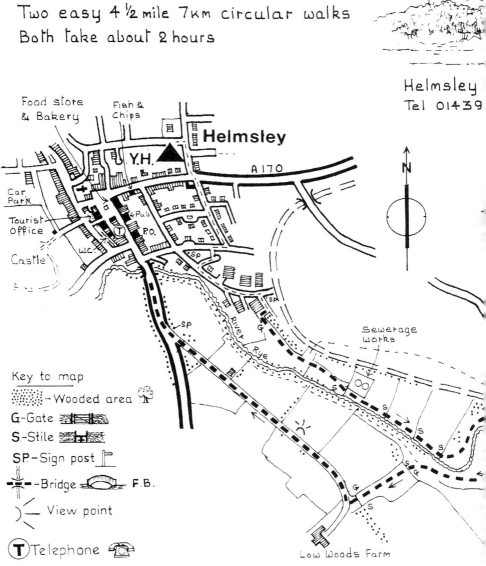

Helmsley
Tel 01439

Food store
& Bakery

Fish &
Chips

Helmsley

Y.H.

A170

N

Car
Park

Tourist
Office

Pub

P.O.

w.c.

Castle

SP

SP

River Rye

SP

G

Sewerage
works

S

S

S

S

Key to map

- Wooded area
G-Gate
S-Stile
SP-Sign post
- Bridge - F.B.
View point
T Telephone

G

S

G

Low Woods Farm

62

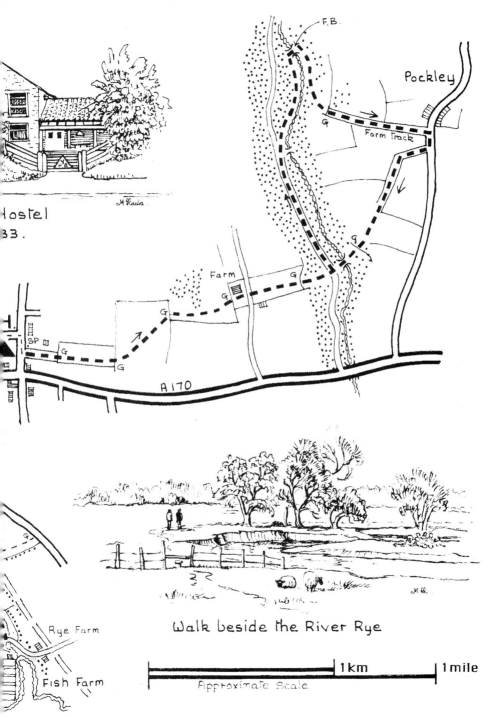

Hostel
33.

Pockley

F.B.

G

Farm Track

G

Farm

G

G

G

SP

G

G

A170

Rye Farm

Fish Farm

G

Walk beside the River Rye

|────────────────────────| 1km ───────| 1 mile

Approximate Scale

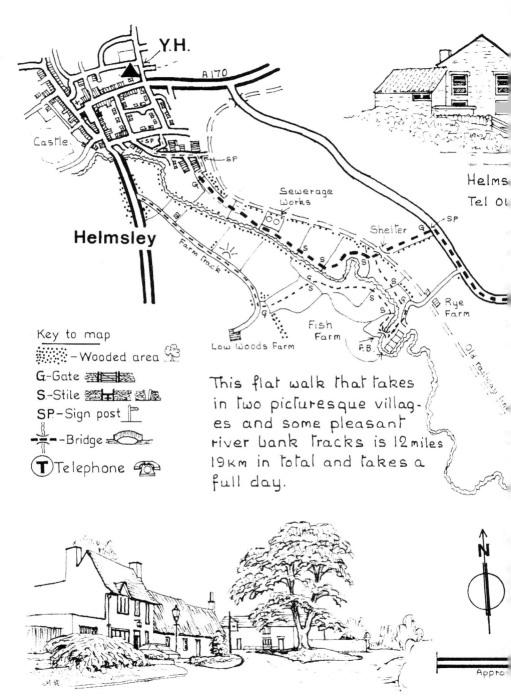

Y.H.

A 170

Castle

Helmsley

Sewerage Works

Shelter

SP

Farm Track

Helms
Tel 01

SP

Rye
Farm

Old railway line

Low Woods Farm

Fish
Farm

F.B.

Key to map
- Wooded area
G-Gate
S.-Stile
SP-Sign post
- Bridge
(T) Telephone

This flat walk that takes
in two picturesque villages and some pleasant
river bank tracks is 12 miles
19km in total and takes a
full day.

N

Appro

The Star Inn Pub at Harome

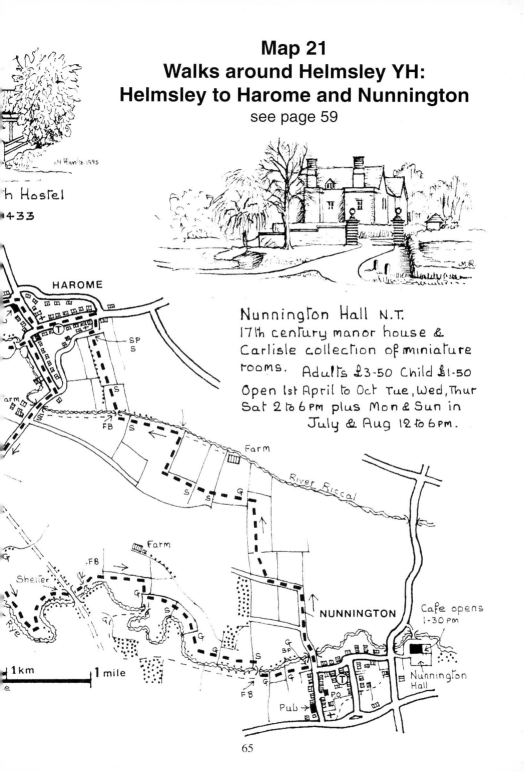

Map 21
Walks around Helmsley YH:
Helmsley to Harome and Nunnington
see page 59

h Hostel

433

HAROME

SP
S

arm

FB S

Nunnington Hall N.T.
17th century manor house &
Carlisle collection of miniature
rooms.   Adults £3-50 Child £1-50
Open 1st April to Oct Tue, Wed, Thur
Sat 2 to 6 pm plus Mon & Sun in
July & Aug 12 to 6 pm.

Farm

River Riccal

Farm

FB

Shelter

Rye

NUNNINGTON

Cafe opens
1-30 pm

1 km   1 mile

Nunnington
Hall

Pub →

Po

Ingleton Youth Hostel (OS Outdoor Leisure Map No 2)

Map 22 (see page 68/69)

Ingleton to Clapham and Ingleborough   12 miles (19km)

This route takes you to the top of Ingleborough at 2,372 feet. It leaves Ingleton for Clapham, progressing through the fields and past Newby village to enter Clapham on an old walled track. The latter has a National Park Information Centre and is a popular village for visitors.

The route to Ingleborough follows Clapdale Wood. There is a nature trail here. Ingleborough Hall was the home of Reginald Farrer, an alpine flower collector and some of his plants may still be seen. The wood is private and a small charge is made.

At the end of the wood is Ingleborough Cave, one of the oldest show caves in the Pennines. The path climbs up through the steep-sided and narrow Trow Gill to reach Gaping Gill — perhaps the most famous cave in Britain. The main pot hole dropping some 360 feet deep. The top of the cave may be slippery and the perimeter fence should not be climbed.

The route becomes steeper as Little Ingleborough is ascended prior to the final climb onto Ingleborough itself. Here, there are magnificent views to be admired before contemplating the descent. The path heads directly to Ingleton. There are a lot of pot holes and even a lead mine in this area. These should be avoided.

Map 23 (See Page 70/71)

Ingleton to Burton-in-Lonsdale   6.5 miles (10km)

Take the B6255 to the A65 and then take the minor road to High Bentham. After passing four fields, the road turns sharp left and the path carries straight on. After crossing several small fields, go past Raygill House, and then the stepping stones, and descend to the River Greta. The path follows the river before joining the minor road (Bentham Moor Road) to reach Burton-in-Lonsdale. The return path is basically down the north side of the River Greta via Lund Farm. Upon reaching the A65, turn right and then left to enter Ingleton.

Map 24 (See Page 72/73)

Ingleton to Masongill   8 miles (12.8km)

This route is only partly on a public right of way and a small toll is payable. The path affected is shown on the map.

The route heads out of Ingleton up the valley of the River Twiss. It crosses the river three times before reaching a track north west of Twisleton Hall. Look out for Pecca Falls and Thornton Force, two waterfalls en route. If you are seeking a short walk, you can turn right upon reaching the lane, walk past Twisleton Hall and return via the River Doe. This alternative is indicated on the map.

For the longer walk, turn left along the track to reach Kingsdale where the path continues by climbing up the steep valley side. At the top is a limestone landscape pittted with shake holes or solution cavities in the limestone. The path reaches an old lane - Turbary Road - and bears left to descend to Masongill. From here there is a pleasant stroll back across the fields to Ingleton.

Keld Youth Hostel (OS Outdoor Leisure Map 30)

Map 25 (see page 74/75)

Keld to Raven Seat   7 miles (11km)

Walk downhill into Keld and cross the River Swale. There are several waterfalls nearby. Kisdon Force is below the footbridge (which is on the Pennine Way). To visit this, turn right just beyond the river. Upstream of the bridge are Catrake Force, best reached from Keld village, plus two other waterfalls reached from West Stonedale, Currack Force and Wain Wath Force.

The path turns west after crossing the River Swale, leaving the Pennine Way at East Stonesdale Farm, just over the river. It then continues up the Swale about 150 feet (50m) above the river before turning up Stonesdale to West Stonesdale.

After returning to Swaledale, the path turns up Whitsun Dale. The path is on the edge of moorland and is not well defined. An alternative and slightly lower path can, however, be used. After reaching Raven Seat, join the minor road and then cross fields to reach the Swale and the B6270 which is followed back to the youth hostel. Look out for Wain Wath Force on the way.

Map 26 (see page 76/77)

Keld to Muker   6.2 miles (10km)

From Keld there is a choice of paths either side of Kisdon Hill. The preferred route on the map is more direct, but the Pennine Way offers views down into Swaledale. Both routes run close to numerous shake holes or drainage holes into the limestone. They should be avoided. The paths join and descend into Muker. In the event of bad weather, the map marks alternative paths which should be used instead. The quickest and easiest is the river valley path beside the Swale between Keld and Muker; or alternatively the path that roughly follows the line of the B6270.

From Muker (well known for its much photographed view from across the bridge to the church), a path leads down to the River Swale and Ivelet Wood. The path runs up the valley close to the river, passing old lead mines at Swinner Gill. Avoid the mines but look for Crackpot Hall, ruined through mining subsidence. The path continues upstream past the impressive Kisdon Force and then East Gill Force to reach Keld.

Map 22   Walks around Ingleton YH:
Ingleton to Clapham and Ingleborough

see page 66

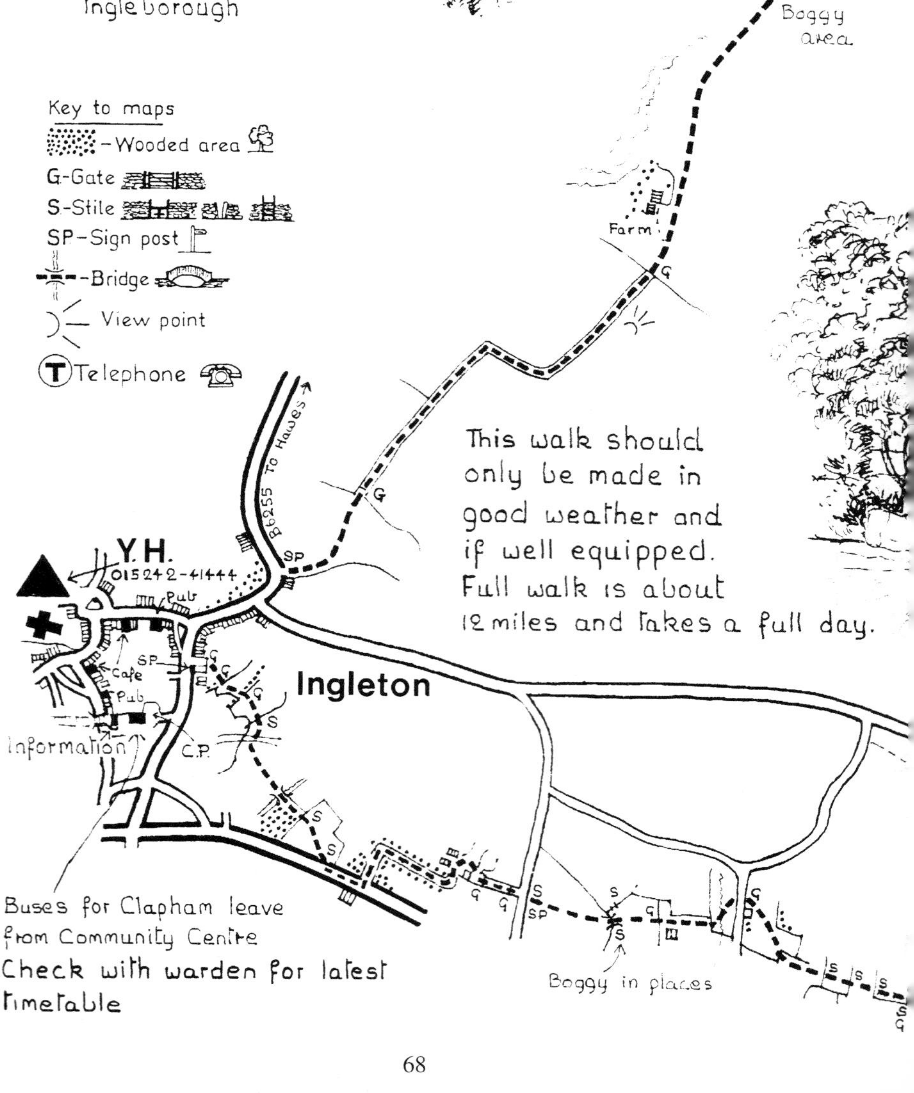

Wind Shelter

Ingleborough

Boggy area

In

Key to maps

- :::: –Wooded area
- G–Gate
- S–Stile
- SP–Sign post
- –Bridge
-)– View point
- (T) Telephone

Farm

G

B6255 To Hawes

G

Y.H.
01524 2-41444

SP

Pub

SP
Cafe
Pub

Information

C.P.

Ingleton

This walk should
only be made in
good weather and
if well equipped.
Full walk is about
12 miles and takes a full day.

S

S
S

S
S
SP
S
S
q q

Buses for Clapham leave
from Community Centre
Check with warden for latest
timetable

Boggy in places

68

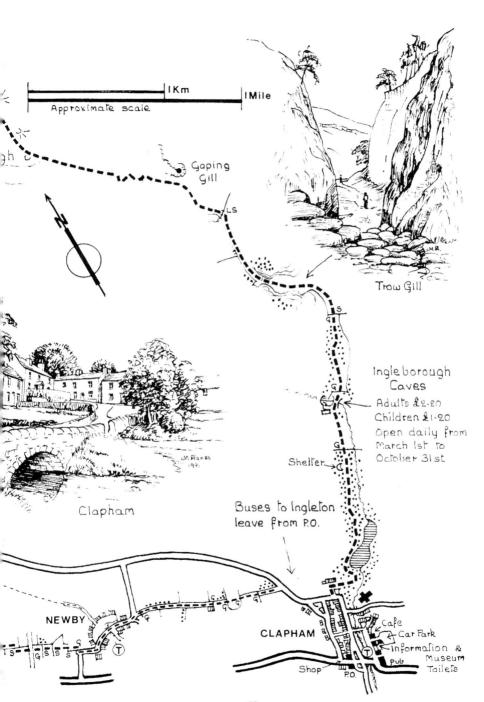

1 Km 1 Mile

Approximate scale

Gaping Gill

LS

Trow Gill

Clapham

Ingleborough Caves
Adults £2·20
Children £1·20
Open daily from
March 1st to
October 31st

Shelter

Buses to Ingleton
leave from P.O.

NEWBY

CLAPHAM

Cafe
Car Park
Information &
Museum
Toilets
Pub
Shop
P.O.

Map 23
Walks around Ingleton YH:
Ingleton to Burton-in-Lonsdale
see page 66

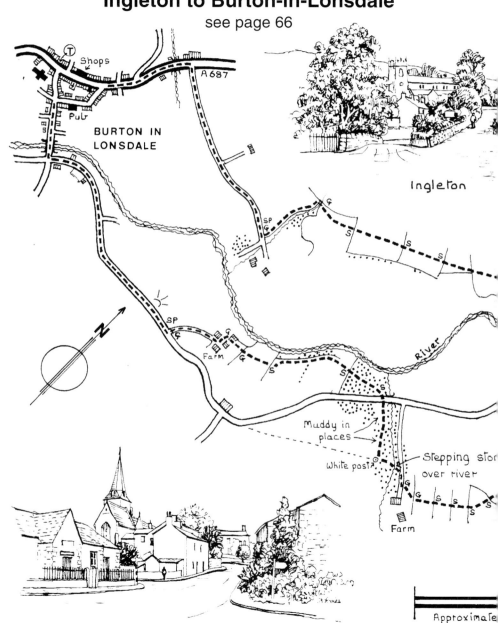

Shops

A 687

Pub

BURTON IN
LONSDALE

Ingleton

SP

SP

Farm

River

Muddy in
places

White post

Stepping stone
over river

Farm

N

Approximate

Burton in Lonsdale

70

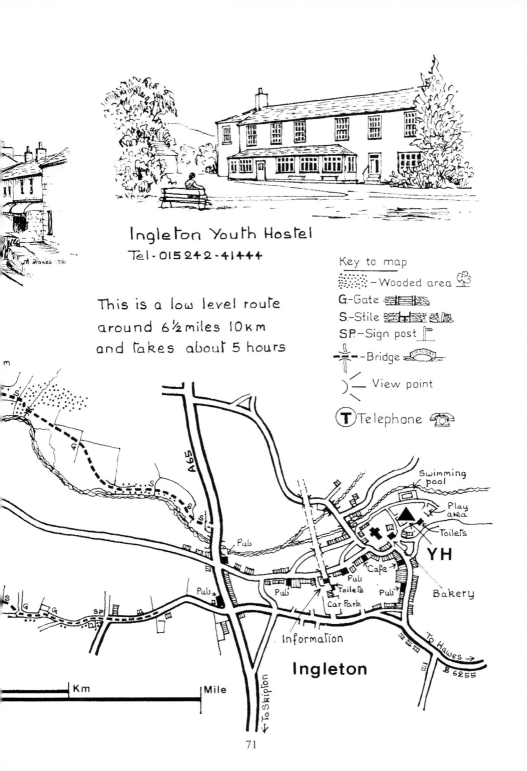

Ingleton Youth Hostel
Tel·015242·41444

This is a low level route
around 6½ miles 10 km
and takes about 5 hours

Key to map
- Wooded area
- G-Gate
- S-Stile
- SP-Sign post
- Bridge
- View point
- T Telephone

Swimming pool
Play area
Toilets
YH
Cafe
Pub
Pub
Bakery
Pub
Pub
Toilets
Car Park
Information
To Hawes
B 6255
Ingleton
A65

Km   Mile

To Skipton

Map 24 Walks around Ingleton YH: Ingleton to Masongill

see page 66

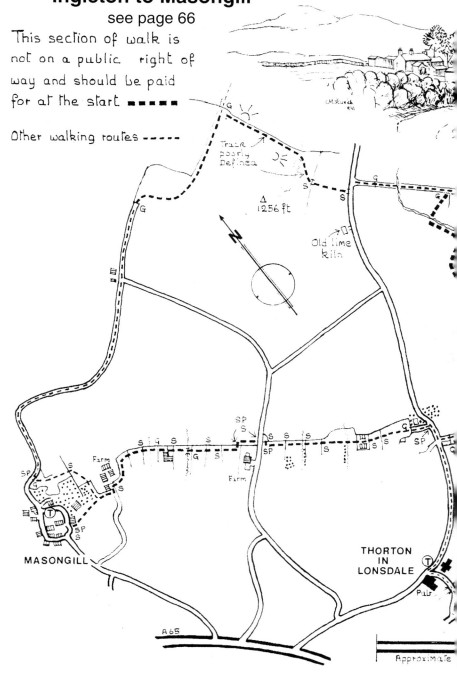

This section of walk is not on a public right of way and should be paid for at the start ▪▪▪▪▪

Other walking routes - - - - -

Train poorly Defined

△ 1256 ft

Old lime kiln

N

G

G

Farm

SP
S

Farm

SP

SP
S

MASONGILL

THORTON IN LONSDALE

Pub

A65

Approximate

72

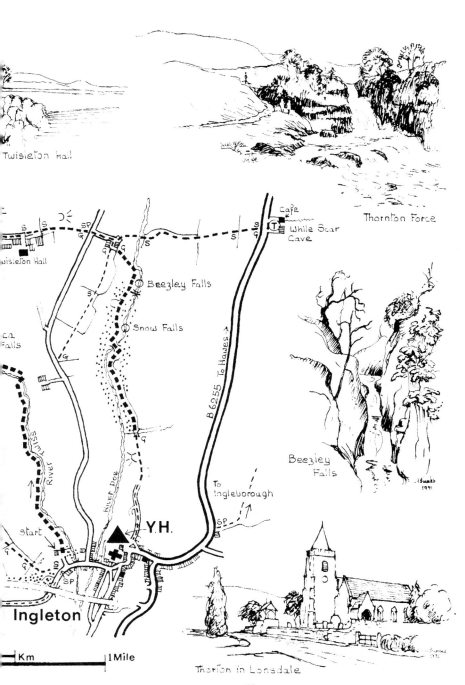

Twisleton Hall

Thornton Force

Twisleton Hall

Café

White Scar Cave

Beezley Falls

Snow Falls

Falls

B 6255 To Hawes →

River Twiss

River Doe

Beezley Falls

A.Banks 1991

To Ingleborough

start

YH.

SP

To Ingleborough

Ingleton

Km   1 Mile

Thornton in Lonsdale

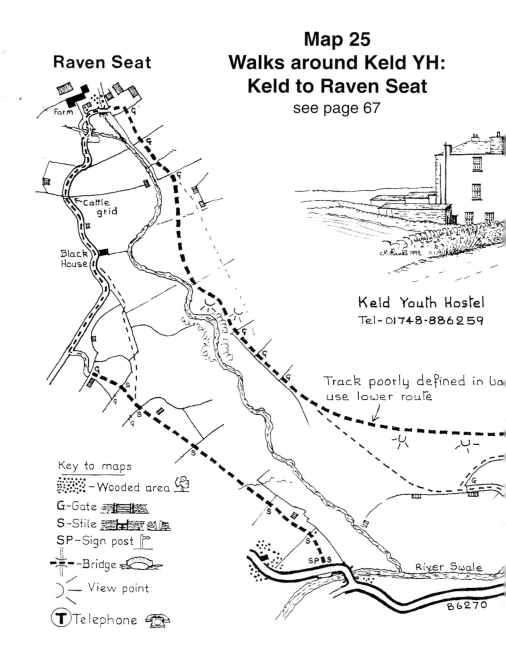

Map 25
Walks around Keld YH:
Keld to Raven Seat
see page 67

Raven Seat

Farm

Cattle grid

Black House

Keld Youth Hostel
Tel- 01748-886259

Track poorly defined in ba
use lower route

Key to maps

░░░ -Wooded area

G-Gate

S-Stile

SP-Sign post

┼─ -Bridge

) — View point

(T) Telephone

River Swale

B6270

This circular day walk up to Raven Seat is about 7miles 11
Please note there is nowhere for refreshments on route.

Other routes - - -

| 1km |
Approximate scale

74

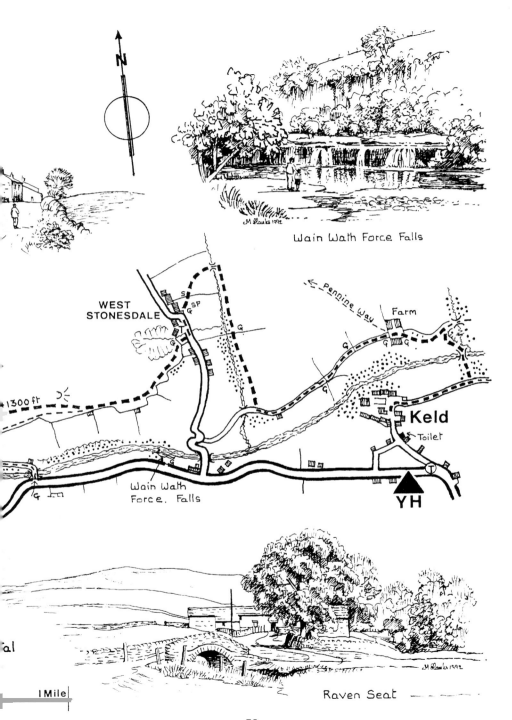

N

Wain Wath Force Falls

WEST
STONESDALE

← Pennine Way

Farm

1300 ft

Keld

Toilet

Wain Wath
Force. Falls

YH

Raven Seat

1 Mile

75

Map 26　Walks around Keld YH:
Keld to Muker
see page 67

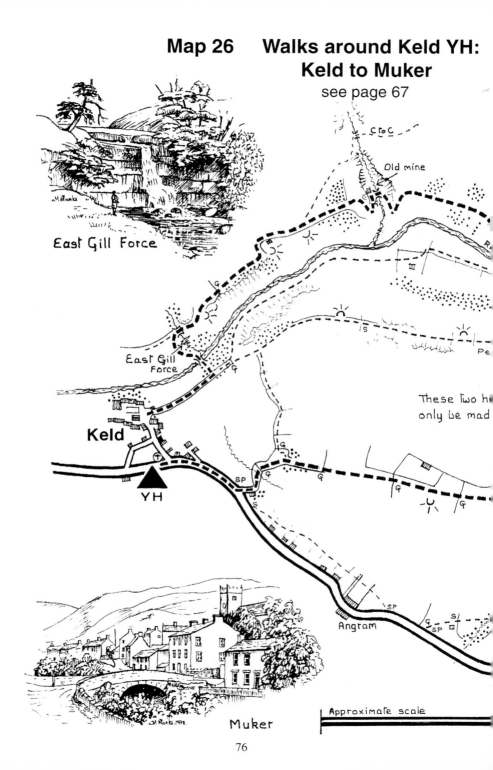

East Gill Force

East Gill Force

CroC

Old mine

East Gill
Force

Keld

YH

SP

These two hi
only be mad

Angram

SP

SP

Approximate scale

Muker

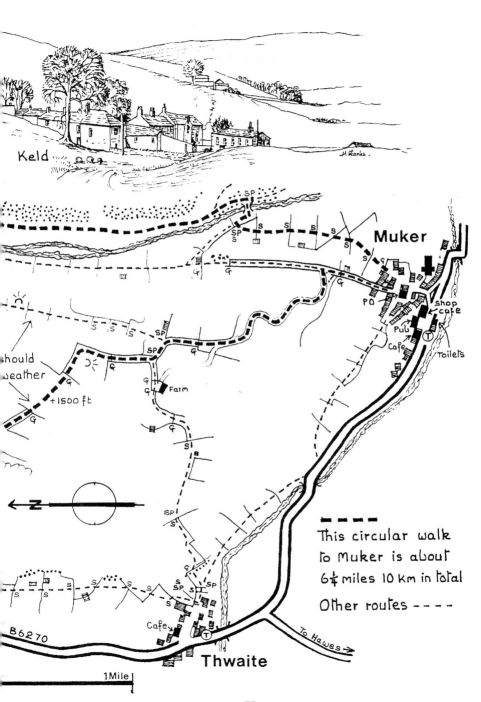

Keld

M Lanks.

Muker

SP
S
SP
S
S
S
S
S
S

G
G
G
G
G
PO
shop
cafe
Pub
Cafe
T
Toilets

n

should
weather

+1500 ft

G
G
G
G
G
G
G
G
Farm

SP
SP

S

S
S
S

Z

SP
S

S
S
S
S
S
SP
S
SP

G
S

Cafe
T

B6270

Thwaite

To Hawes →

This circular walk to Muker is about 6¼ miles 10 km in total

Other routes - - - -

1 Mile

77

Kettlewell Youth Hostel

Map 27 (see page 80/81)

Kettwell to Arncliffe and Hawkswick   7 miles (11Km)

After crossing the River Wharfe, the path climbs steadily out of Wharfedale onto Old Cote Little Moor. Avoid the shake holes in the limestone en route. From the top of the path, it drops down to the River Skirfare through Byre Bank Wood to reach Arncliffe, where there is a pub and cafe.

From here, the path to Hawkswick starts by the eighteenth century church, running through the river meadows all the way. The river is crossed on a footbridge just before reaching the hamlet, turning left to climb up to the moor again with views down into Wharfedale beyond the confluence with the River Skirfare. Upon reaching the high ground, the path runs downhill directly to Kettlewell, joining the B6160 just outside the village.

Kirkby Stephen Youth Hostel

Map 28 (see page 82/83)

Kirkby Stephen to Pendragon Castle   9 miles (14.5km)

The paths starts from near to the huge parish church, which is well worth a visit. The route follows a lane to Nateby, passing Stenkrith Falls which are just below the road bridge over the River Eden. Beyond Nateby, the path heads down to the river and the ruins of Wharton Hall. Here the path branches. Continue to walk up-river through the fields to reach the remains of Pendragon Castle. This is a Normal peel tower, rebuilt in 1660 but now ruinous. From here, a lane climbs away from the river which is followed before heading northwards back to Wharton Hall. A lane can be taken to reach the A685 Sedbergh - Kirkby Stephen road; otherwise retrace your steps back through Nateby.

Note the short walk on the map down to Hartley and along the old railway track, returning via Winton.

Map 29 (see page 84/85)

Kirkby Stephen to Ravenstonedale   10.5 miles (16.7km)

Take the lane behind the youth hostel in a westerly direction over an old railway line. Look out for yellow painted posts waymarking the route. A mile after crossing another (and still used) railway line, the path turns south to Ravenstonedale. In addition to an interesting church, the village has perhaps the best bookshop in the country devoted to industrial/railway history. Run by Chris Irwin, it is called The Book House.

      From the village a path heads for Smardale Bridge. Just beyond here, it joins the abandoned railway, crossing a huge viaduct. The lane runs above the Scandal Beck before turning towards Smardale Hall. Lanes are taken to beyond Waitby, back over the disused railway before a final path leads back into Kirkby Stephen.

Linton Youth Hostel (OS Outdoor Leisure Map 10)

Map 30 (see page 86/87)

Linton to Burnsall   6.5 miles (10.3km)

From the delightful setting of Linton village, the path goes first to Linton church before turning upriver to cross the River Wharfe by Linton Falls and reaching the Dales Way. Alternatively, stepping stones can be used a little downstream from the church. The path follows the river all the way to Burnsall, changing riverbank near Hebden.

      A path returns via Thorpe (which is a Viking name meaning small village) back to Linton.

Notice the various circular routes on the map which can be used as an evening stroll.

Map 31 (see page 88/89)

Linton to Gregory Wood, Wharfedale   6.5 miles (10.3km)

This route crosses the River Wharfe as in the last walk i.e. either via St Michael's Church or directly down to Linton Falls. A diversion in Grassington may be made, otherwise, turn upstream on the River Wharfe. It reaches Gregory Wood, which covers Far Gregory and Dewbottom Scar. The path leaves the valley at the far end of the wood, climbing a little before reaching the Canistone - Grassington path. This is used for the return to Grassington, entering the village on the Dales Way. The Upper Wharfedale Folk Museum is situated here, along with a National Park Information Centre.

Map 27
Walks around Kettlewell YH:
Kettlewell to Arncliffe and Hawkswick
see page 78

Approximate distance of circular route
7miles 11km in total — — —

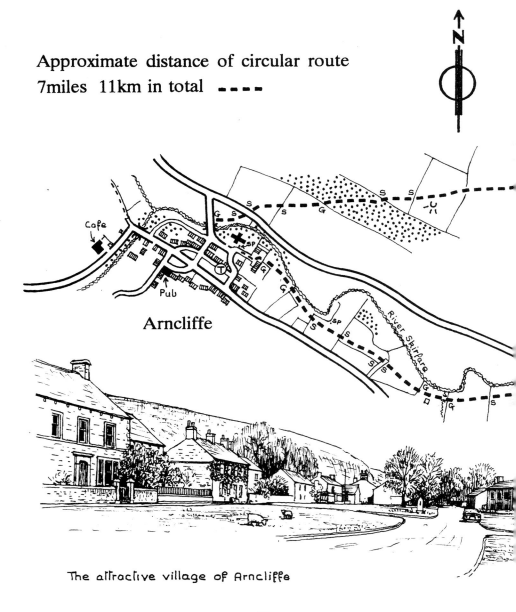

Arncliffe

The attractive village of Arncliffe

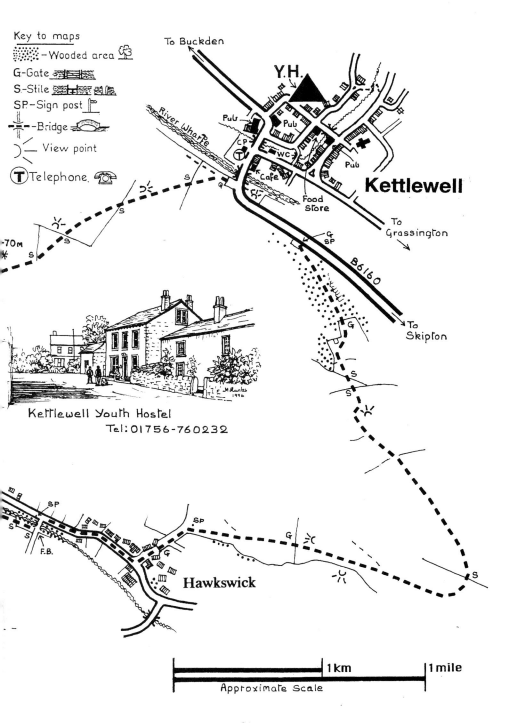

Key to maps
⬚⬚⬚ – Wooded area 🌳
G – Gate
S – Stile
SP – Sign post
– Bridge
)— View point
(T) Telephone.

To Buckden

Y.H.

River Wharfe

Pub
Pub
CP
WC
Cafe
Food Store

Kettlewell

To Grassington

-70M

G
SP

B6160

To Skipton

G

S
S

Kettlewell Youth Hostel
Tel: 01756 - 760232

E. M. Banks
1996

SP

SP
G

F.B.

G

S

Hawkswick

1 km   1 mile
Approximate Scale

Map 28
Walks around Kirkby Stephen YH:
Kirkby Stephen to Pendragon Castle
see page 78

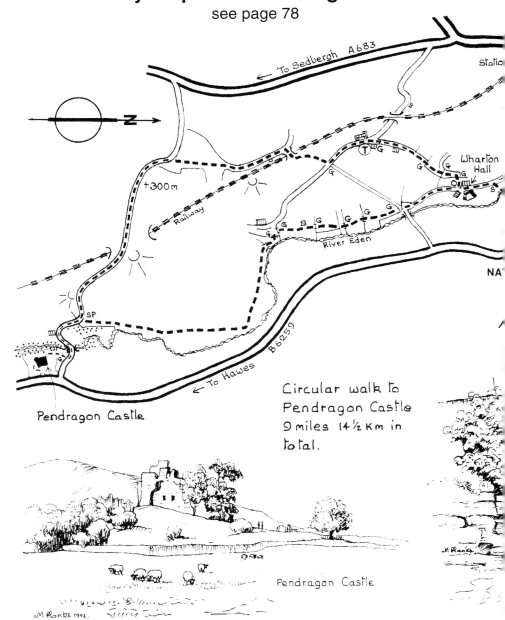

To Sedbergh A683

Station

Wharton Hall

+300m

Railway

River Eden

NA

SP

B6259

To Hawes

Pendragon Castle

Circular walk to
Pendragon Castle
9 miles 14½ Km in
total.

Pendragon Castle

M Ranks 1991.

Approximate scale

1Km   1Mile

Kirkby Stephen Hostel
Tel-01768-371793

M Ranks 1991

A685

Pub

shop
Cafe
SP

SP

G

Car Park

YH.

Pub

Stenkrith
Falls

SP

SP

Information
Office

G
SP

W.C.

Kirkby
Stephen

To Brough

A685

G

T

HARTLEY

G

Quarry

S
G

old railway

Pub

WINTON

T

Key to map

:::::::: — Wooded area

G-Gate

S-Stile

S.P.-Sign post

— Bridge

) (— View point

T Telephone

h Falls

83

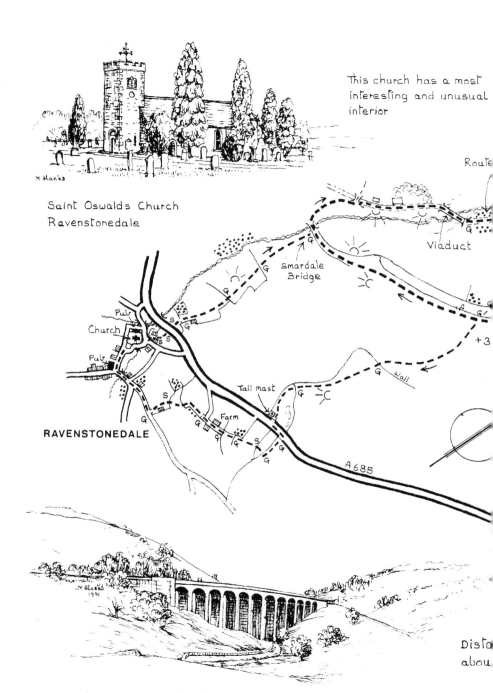

This church has a most interesting and unusual interior

Saint Oswalds Church
Ravenstonedale

Route

Viaduct

Smardale
Bridge

Pub
Church
Pub

Tall mast
RAVENSTONEDALE
Farm

Wall

+3

A685

Dista
abou

Viaduct crossed on old railway route

see page 79

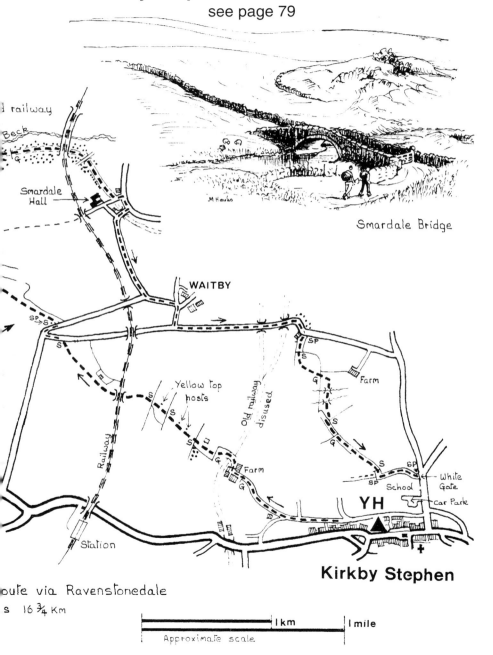

Smardale Bridge

M Hauko

route via Ravenstonedale

s 16 ¾ Km

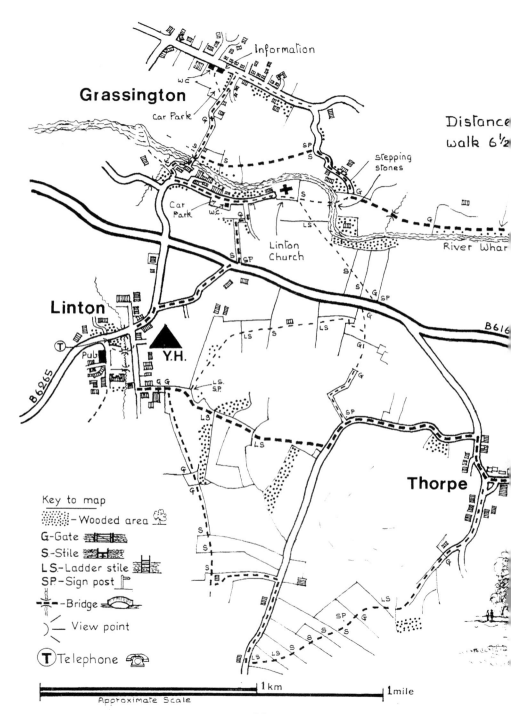

Grassington

Information

Distance
walk 6½

w.c.

Car Park

Stepping
Stones

River Whar

Car
Park

w.c.

Linton
Church

B616

Linton

B6265

Pub

Y.H.

LS
S.P.

Thorpe

LS

LS

Key to map

::::: – Wooded area

G – Gate

S – Stile

LS – Ladder stile

SP – Sign post

⊣•⊢ – Bridge

)⟍— View point

(T) Telephone

1 km   1 mile

Approximate Scale

86

Map 30   Walks around Linton YH:
Linton to Burnsall see page 79

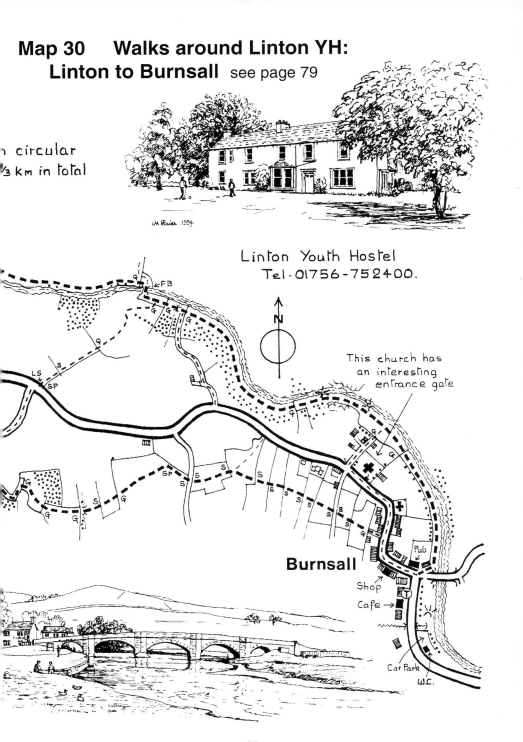

a circular
3 km in total

Linton Youth Hostel
Tel· 01756-752400.

This church has
an interesting
entrance gate

Burnsall

Shop
Cafe →

Pub

Car Park
W.C.

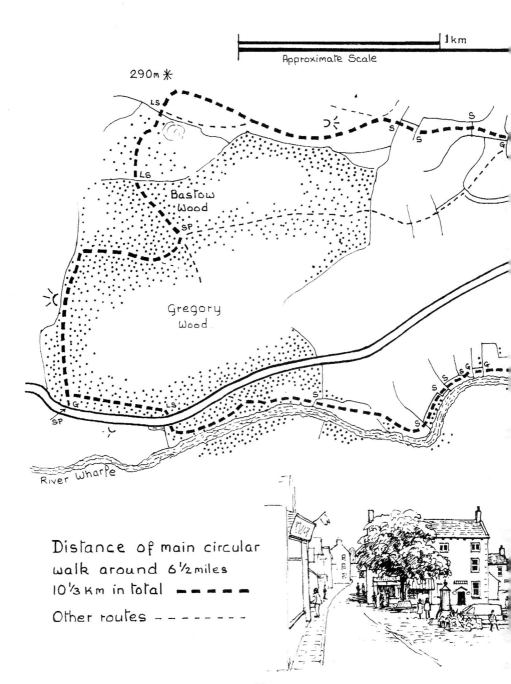

1km

Approximate Scale

290m ✳

LS

LS

Bastow
Wood

SP

LS

Gregory
Wood

S

S

S

S

G

S

G

G

S

S

S

G

G

S

S

G

SP

LS

River Wharfe

Distance of main circular
walk around 6½ miles
10⅓ km in total ▬ ▬ ▬ ▬

Other routes ‑ ‑ ‑ ‑ ‑ ‑ ‑

Map 31   Walks around Linton YH:
Linton to Gregory Wood, Wharfedale

see page 79

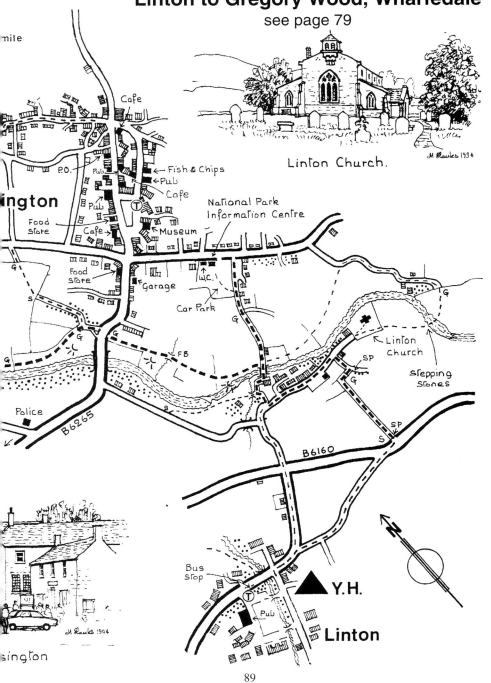

Linton Church.

M Rawles 1994

mile

Cafe

P.O.   Pub   ← Fish & Chips
              ← Pub
                Cafe

ington   Pub   National Park
                     Information Centre
Food
Store   Cafe →   Museum

Food
Store   Garage
         Car Park   W.C.

              FB   Linton
                    Church

                    Stepping
                    Stones

Police   SP

B6265   SP
         B6160

Bus
Stop   ▲ Y.H.

M Rawles 1994   Pub   **Linton**

sington

89

Lockton Youth Hostel

Map 32 (see page 92/93)

Lockton to Low Dalby   6.5 miles (10.5km)

Cross the road towards Levisham and join the path which heads south to the North
Yorkshire Moors Railway. This is a preserved line running into the moors from Pickering.
The path switches direction here, climbing out of Newton Dale and heading for the Fox
and Rabbit Inn. A path continues past the pub to reach Dalby Forest at High Dalby. Here a
woodland path can be taken to reach the Forest Visitors' Centre at Low Dalby. Retracing
your steps to High Dalby, there is a short walk back into Lockton.

This circular walk may be extended by turning right just north of High Dalby and
walking along Stain Dale to High Staindale, returning via Low Pasture Farm and Green
Dale. There are forest walks from High Staindale and from the Dalby Visitor Centre.

Map 33 (see page 94/95)

Locton to Saltergate   8 miles (12.7km)

Take the road from Lockton to the nearby village of Levisham and then the lane which
bears to the right of the pub. The lane climbs uphill to Levisham Moor passing Dundale
Pond. There is a well defined path across the moor to Saltergate and good views across the
moors. The path returns by the Hole of Horcum. This basin is drained by the Levisham
Beck. On the south side, the valley becomes very narrow. After crossing the Beck, the
path enters an area of dense scrub and the track is in places a little overgrown.

This walk may be extended by heading south east towards Dalby Forest and Stain
Dale across Lockton Low Moor. Look out for the Bridestones, sandstone outcrops to the
right of the main path. A track enables you to reach them. This extension to the walk adds
on another 1.5miles (2.25km)

Malham Youth Hostel (OS Outdoor Leisure Map 10)

Map 34 (see page 96/97)

Malham to Kirkby Malham   4.2m (6.5km)

A track from the end of Chapel Gate leads up onto the lower flank of Kirkby Fell. This is followed before turning Southwest to pass Accraplates Farm at the head of Tranlands Gill. From here, the path heads for Cow Close Lane which runs down into Kirkby Malham. Here the area's first church was built in the eighth century, of which perhaps the name Chapel Gate at Malham is a reminder.

The path to Malham drops down to the river Aire and runs along the river bank or through the meadows back to the village.

Note the short evening walk marked on the map.

Map 35 (see page 98/99)

Malham to Malham Tarn   7.2 miles (11km)

Follow the river downstream before bearing to the left by a stream and heading for Wedber Wood. At the far end of this is Janet's Foss, a picturesque waterfall. Notice the nature trail in the wood which may be of interest. Crossing Gardale Lane, the path heads for Gardale Scar. Don't be too put off at the thought of climbing up this waterfall. It is fairly easy if you go up the left hand side. Alternatively, use the path shown on the map to reach the tarn by a different and easier route.

Pass through the scree at the top of the waterfall and then through the boulder-strewn field to reach the road. The tarn lies ahead and you can get down to the water if you bear to the right (on the Pennine Way).

The path back to Malham crosses the road once more. The route passes an area full of shake holes, one of which takes the stream issuing from the tarn. It reappears further on at the foot of Malham Cove. Continue down the valley to reach the limestone pavement above the cave and the dramatic view of the latter, as the path zig-zags down to the bottom. Watch you feet on crossing the pavement!

From the cave, there is a well trodden path back to the village.

Map 32
Walks around Lockton YH:
Lockton to Low Dalby
see page 90

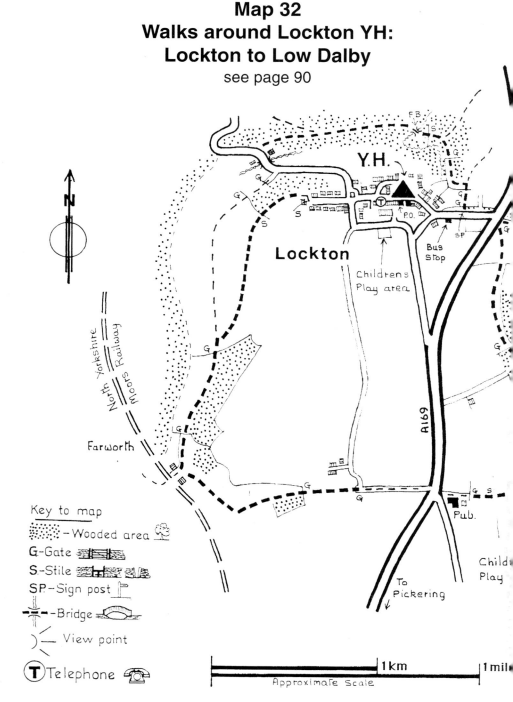

Y.H.

Lockton

Farworth

North Yorkshire Moors Railway

Childrens
Play area

Bus
Stop

A169

P.O.

Pub.

Child
Play

To
Pickering

Key to map

- Wooded area

G-Gate

S.-Stile

SP-Sign post

- Bridge

View point

T Telephone

1km   1 mile

Approximate Scale

92

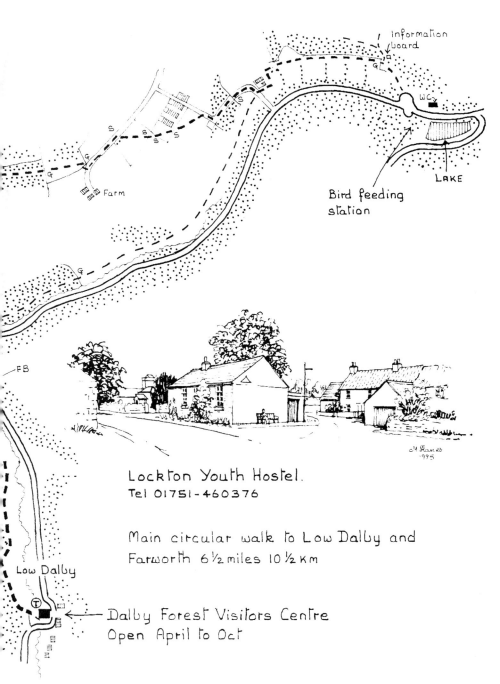

Information
board

WC₅

LAKE

Bird feeding
station

Farm

FB

Lockton Youth Hostel.
Tel 01751-460376

Main circular walk to Low Dalby and
Farworth 6 ½ miles 10 ½ km

Low Dalby

Dalby Forest Visitors Centre
Open April to Oct

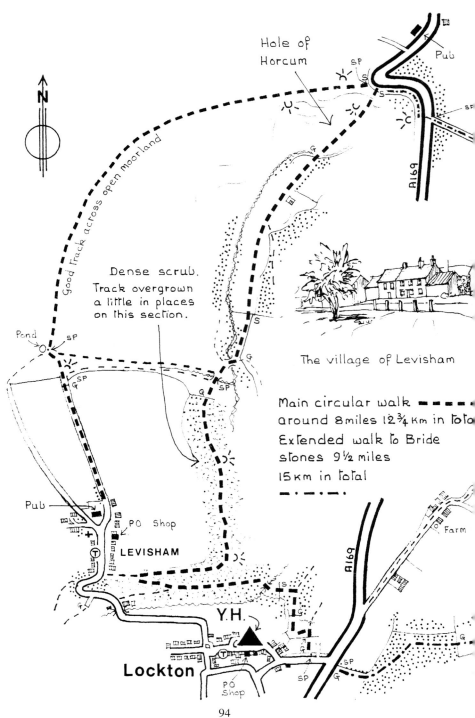

Hole of Horcum

Pub

A169

SP

Good Track across open Moorland

Dense scrub. Track overgrown a little in places on this section.

Pond SP

The village of Levisham

Main circular walk ■ ■ ■
around 8 miles 12¾ Km in total
Extended walk to Bride stones 9½ miles
15 km in total
■ ─ ■ ─ ■

Pub

PO Shop

LEVISHAM

Y.H.

Lockton

PO Shop

Farm

A169

Map 33 Walks around Lockton YH: Lockton to Saltergate

see page 90

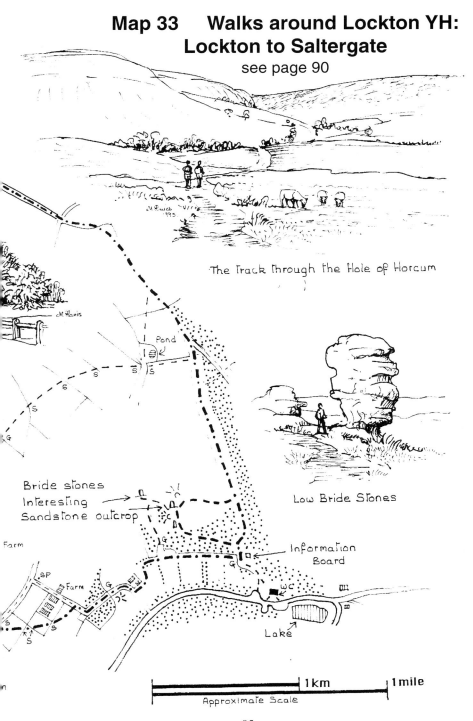

The Track Through the Hole of Horcum

Low Bride Stones

Bride stones
Interesting →
Sandstone outcrop

Farm

Pond

Information
Board

Farm

Lake

| 1km | 1mile |

Approximate Scale

Map 34
Walks around Malham YH:
Malham to Kirkby Malham
see page 91

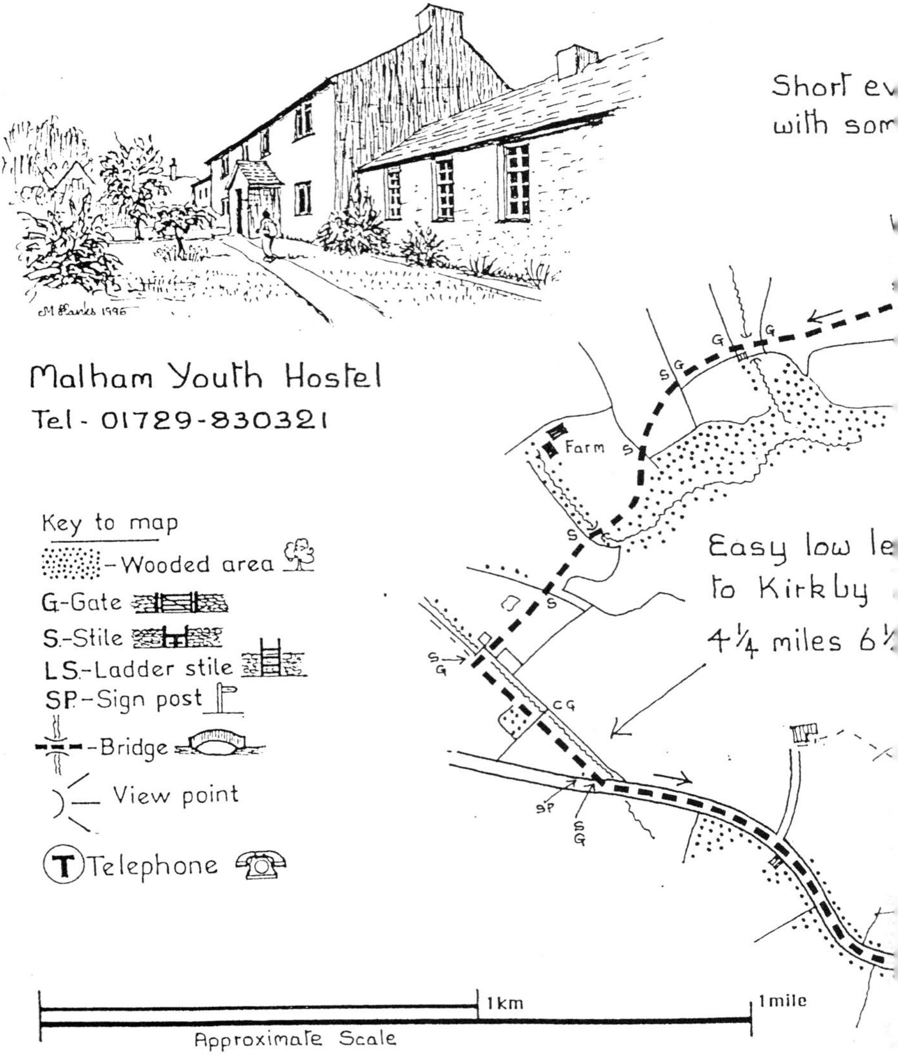

Malham Youth Hostel
Tel - 01729-830321

Short ev
with som

Farm

Easy low le
to Kirkby
4¼ miles 6½

Key to map
[illustration] - Wooded area 🌳
G - Gate [illustration]
S. - Stile [illustration]
LS. - Ladder stile [illustration]
SP - Sign post [illustration]
✦ - Bridge [illustration]
) - View point
(T) Telephone ☎

| | 1km | 1 mile |
Approximate Scale

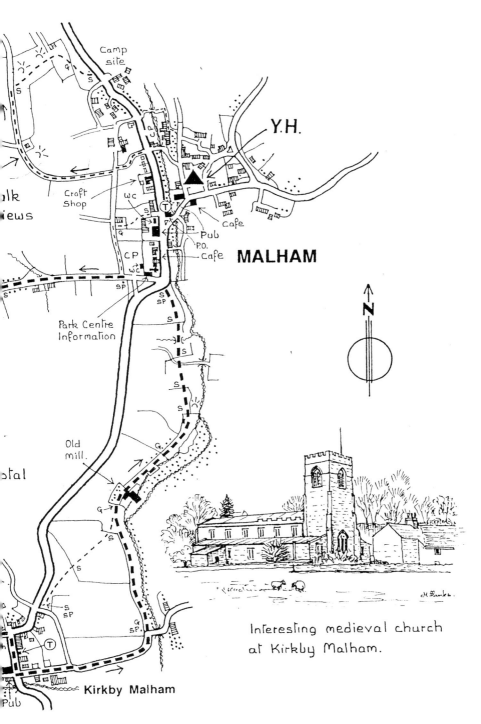

Camp
site

Y.H.

Craft
Shop

wc

Cafe

Pub
P.O.
Cafe

MALHAM

N

Park Centre
Information

Old
mill.

Interesting medieval church
at Kirkby Malham.

Kirkby Malham

Map 35   Walks around Malham YH:
Malham to Malham Tarn

see page 91

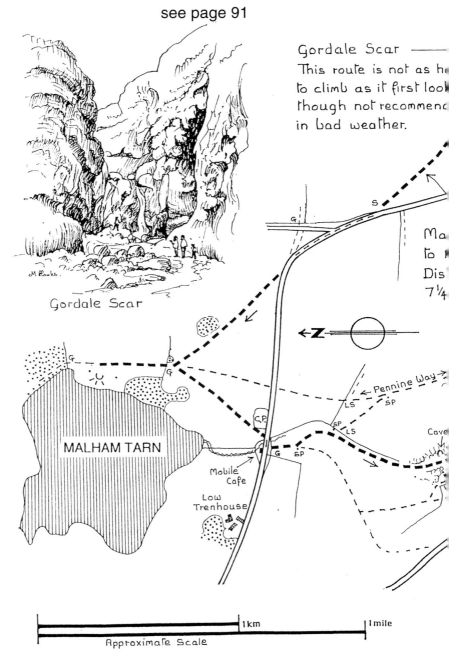

Gordale Scar

Gordale Scar ———
This route is not as he
to climb as it first loo
though not recommenc
in bad weather.

←**Z**

Ma
to
Dis
7¼

←Pennine Way→

LS   SP

SP
SP   LS   Cave

LS

C.P.

MALHAM TARN

G   SP

Mobile
Cafe

Low
Trenhouse

|————————————————————————|1km |1mile
Approximate Scale

98

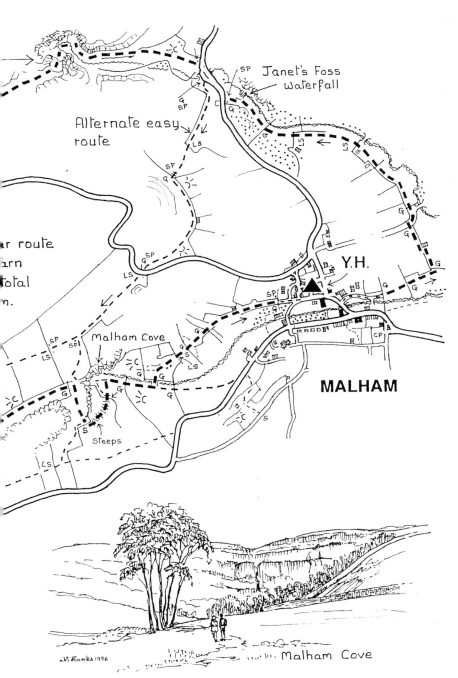

Janet's Foss Waterfall

Alternate easy route

r route
arn
total
n.

Malham Cove

Y.H.

MALHAM

Steeps

M Banks 1996

Malham Cove

Mankinholes Youth Hostel

Map 36 (see page 102/103)

Mankinholes to Cragg Vale   8 miles (12km)

Climb the moor behind the hostel before dropping down to Withens Clough Reservoir on a track which leads to Cragg Vale, set in a wooded area on the B6138 Littleborough to Mytholmroyd Road. The path then joins a track which zig-zags up towards the moor again. Part of the route can be boggy and an alternative route to avoid this is shown on the plan

   The route passes Stoodley Pike, built to commemorate the Battle of Waterloo. The views from this area are extensive. Note the alternative and much shorter circular route shown on the map.

   From near to the hostel, look down the valley to the west. There is a tall building visible which is a waterwheel house to a demolished cotton mill. This had an unusual arrangement of three wheels arranged vertically, the water dropping from one waterwheel directly onto another beneath it.

Map 37 (see page 104/105)

Mankinholes to Todmorden   4.5 miles (7km)

This short route drops down to the canal in the Calder Valley. It is a picturesque walk along the tow path to Todmorden where a lane rises past the church. Take this and after about 1/2 mile, turn left to cross through the fields back to Mankinholes. There are extensive views in all directions on this section of the route. Upon reaching the hamlet of Lubutts, you can proceed directly to the hostel past the pub or go up the road past the church.

Map 38 (see page 106/107)

Mankinholes to Hebden Bridge   12 miles (19.2km)

This circular route may be shortened by 4 miles (6.5km) by ignoring the extension of the path into Hebden Bridge. Alternatively, you can visit there on foot and return to Lobb Mill on the Todmorden Road (A646) by bus. There are also buses direct to Mankinholes every two hours. If you prefer to walk, you can return along the canal towpath, turning uphill towards Mankinholes at a choice of three places.

   A 7.7 mile (12.5km) walk following paths referred to above can be extended north of the A646 with good views back towards Stoodley Pike and Mankinholes.

Osmotherley Youth Hostel (OS Outdoor Leisure Map 2)

Map 39 (see page 108/109)

Osmotherley to Mount Grace Priory 2.5 miles (4km)

This short walk crosses fields before descending steeply through a wood to emerge at Mount Grace Priory. Built in 1398 by the Carthusian Order, it is now owned by English Heritage and quite a lot of it survives. It looks particularly attractive in spring time, when the daffodils are in flower. Upon returning to the fields above and reaching Chapel Wood Farm, you can turn left onto the Cleveland Way. Upon reaching a gate bear right up past a wood to reach a lane and two alternative ways back to the Youth Hostel. Both are marked on the map.

Map 40 (see page 110/111)

Osmotherley to Chequers Farm 4.5 miles (7.25km)

From the hostel turn right and proceed through the adjacent wood to reach a lane. Turn right and after a mile, Chequers Farm is reached, where there is a cafe. Continue another mile to where the road bears left. Here a path is signposted to the right. Take this past two small reservoirs and cross the fields back into the village. Osmotherley is unusual in having a pub named after Queen Catherine. The youth hostel formerly made ships sails and is thought to have made sails for Captain Cook who came from this district.

Scarborough Youth Hostel

Map 41 (see page 112/113)

Scarborough to Hayburn Wyke 10.25 miles (16.5km)

The cliffs near to Scarborough are famed for the magnificent views and this coastal path enables you to enjoy them to the full. For a shorter walk of 7.75 miles (12.5km), you can leave the outbound path at Cloughton and walk directly to the sea to pick up the coastal path at that point.

The route follows the A165 for about a mile to the outskirts of Burniston, where it joins a path along an old railway line. After 2.5 miles (4km) the road turns away from the old line and heads for the coast to return to the hostel along the coastal path. Upon reaching the headland on the near side of North Bay, turn right and the hostel is directly ahead of you.

Map 36
Walks around Mankinholes YH:
Mankinholes to Cragg Vale

see page 100

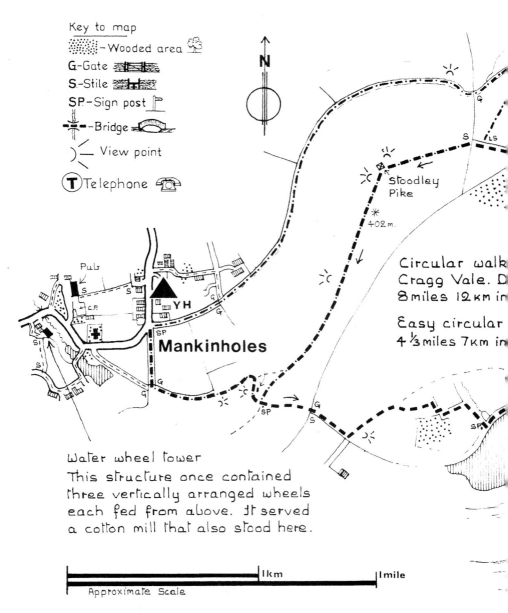

Key to map

::::: – Wooded area 🌳
G–Gate
S–Stile
SP–Sign post
––Bridge
)– View point
(T) Telephone

N

Stoodley Pike

*402 m.

Circular walk
Cragg Vale. D
8 miles 12 km in

Easy circular
4 ⅓ miles 7 km in

YH

Mankinholes

Pub

SP

G

Water wheel tower
This structure once contained
three vertically arranged wheels
each fed from above. It served
a cotton mill that also stood here.

|————————————————————| 1km | 1mile
Approximate Scale

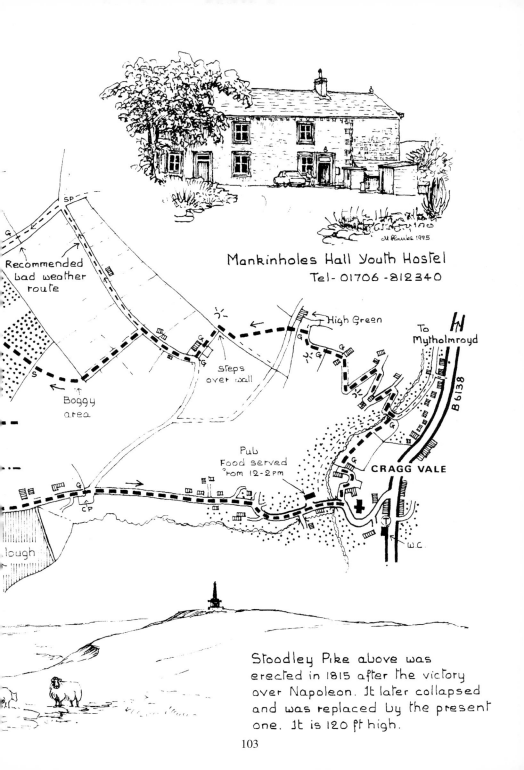

M. Fowles 1995

Mankinholes Hall Youth Hostel
Tel- 01706 -812340

SP

Recommended
bad weather
route

←High Green

To
Mytholmroyd

B6138

Boggy
area

Steps
over wall

Pub
Food served
from 12-2pm

CRAGG VALE

CP

lough

W.C.

Stoodley Pike above was
erected in 1815 after the victory
over Napoleon. It later collapsed
and was replaced by the present
one. It is 120 ft high.

Map 37   Walks around Mankinholes YH: Mankinholes to Todmorden

see page 100

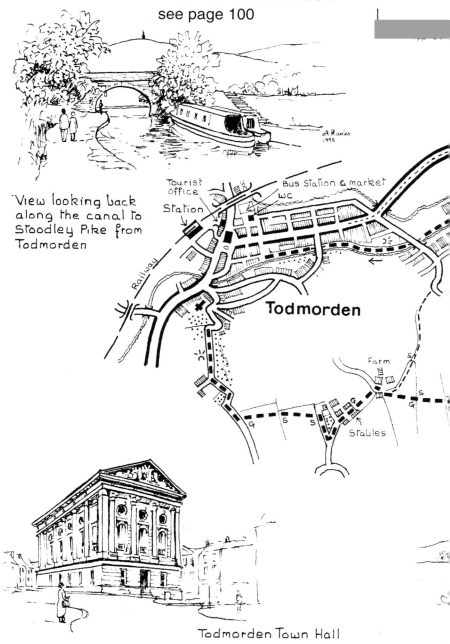

View looking back along the canal to Stoodley Pike from Todmorden

Todmorden

Todmorden Town Hall

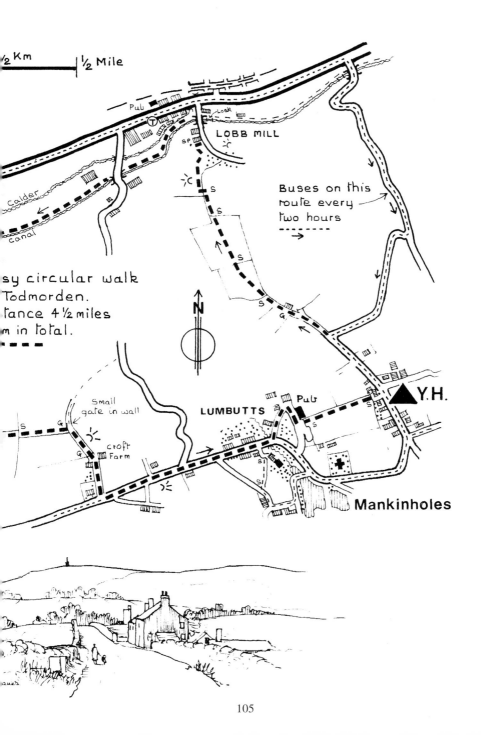

½ Km ½ Mile

Pub
Lobb
LOBB MILL

Calder
canal

Buses on this
route every
two hours
→

sy circular walk
Todmorden.
tance 4½ miles
m in total.

N

Small
gate in wall

Croft
Farm

LUMBUTTS

Pub

Y.H.

Mankinholes

105

Map 38 Walks around Mankinholes YH:
Mankinholes to Hebden Bridge

see page 100

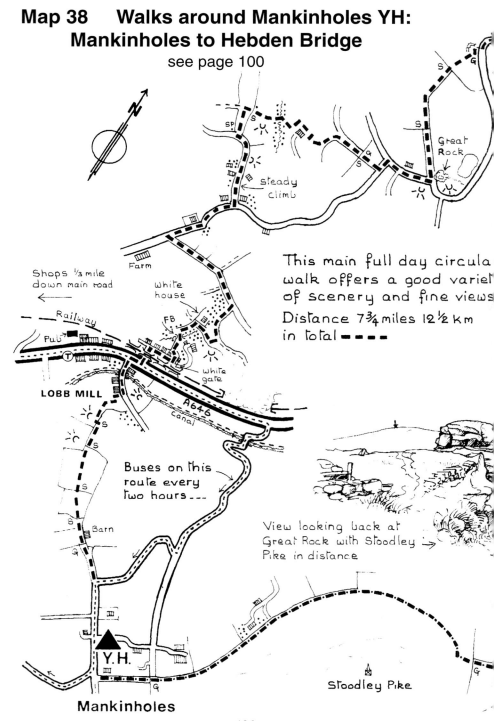

Great Rock

SP

steady climb

Farm

Shops ⅓ mile down main road ←

White house

Railway

Pub

T

LOBB MILL

FB

White gate

A646

Canal

This main full day circula walk offers a good variet of scenery and fine views

Distance 7¾ miles 12½ km in total ▬ ▬ ▬

Buses on this route every two hours ▬ ▬ ▬

Barn

View looking back at Great Rock with Stoodley Pike in distance →

Y.H.

Stoodley Pike

Mankinholes

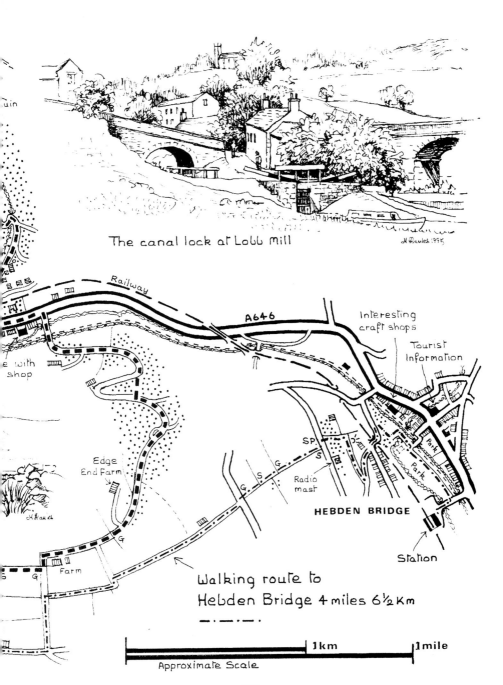

The canal lock at Lobb mill

H. Hawkes 1995

Railway

A646

Interesting
craft shops

Tourist
Information

e with
shop

Edge
End Farm

SP

S
G
G
S
G

Radio
mast

Park
Park

HEBDEN BRIDGE

Farm

G
G

S

Station

Walking route to
Hebden Bridge 4 miles 6½ Km

1km   1mile

Approximate Scale

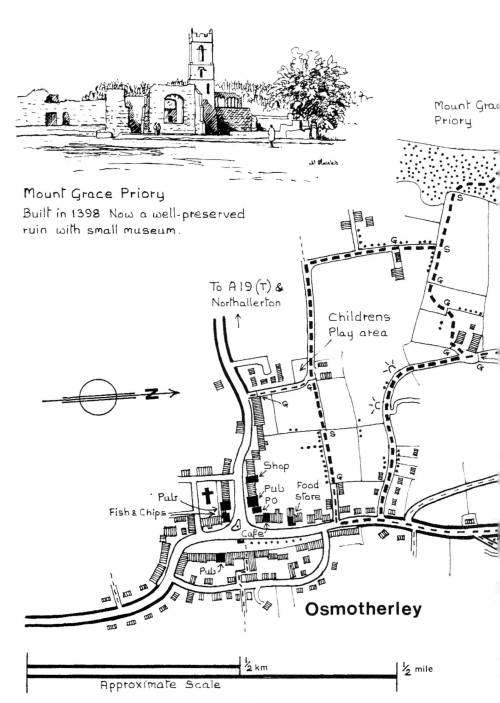

Mount Grace Priory

Mount Grace Priory
Built in 1398 Now a well-preserved
ruin with small museum.

To A19 (T) &
Northallerton

Childrens
Play area

N

Shop

Pub
PO

Food
Store

Pub

Fish & Chips

Cafe

Pub

Osmotherley

½ km   ½ mile

Approximate Scale

Map 39
Walks around Osmotherley YH:
Osmotherley to Mount Grace Priory
see page 101

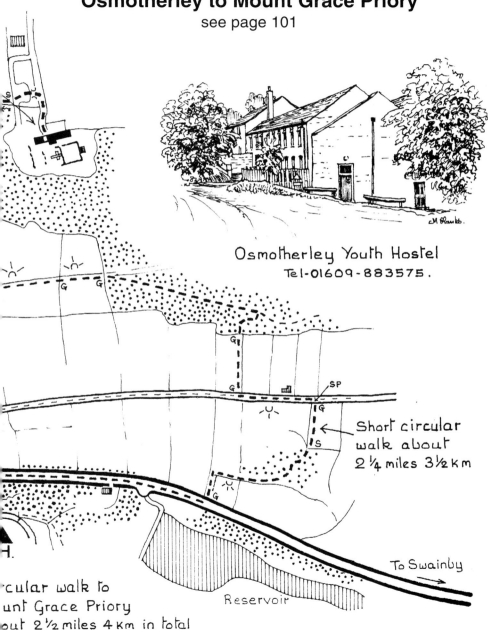

Osmotherley Youth Hostel
Tel·01609·883575.

SP

Short circular
walk about
2¼ miles 3½ km

To Swainby

Reservoir

·cular walk to
unt Grace Priory
out 2½ miles 4 km in total

Map 40 Walks around Osmotherley YH: Osmotherley to Chequers Farm

see page 101

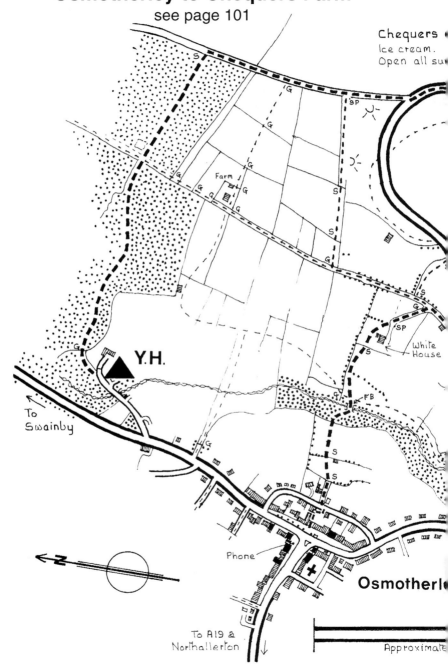

Chequers
Ice cream.
Open all su

Farm

White
House

FB

Y.H.

To
Swainby

Phone

Osmotherl

To A19 &
Northallerton

Approximate

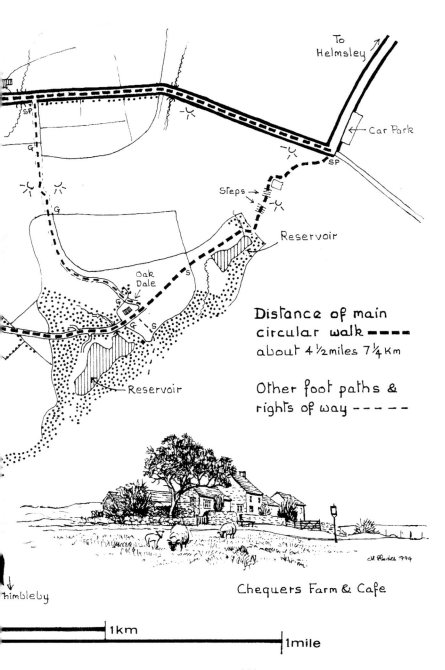

To Helmsley

SP

← Car Park

SP

Steps →

Reservoir

Oak Dale

S

G

G

S

Reservoir

Distance of main
circular walk ▬ ▬ ▬ ▬
about 4 ½ miles 7 ¼ Km

Other foot paths &
rights of way - - - -

Chequers Farm & Cafe

M Plawes 1994

↓ Thimbleby

1km

1mile

111

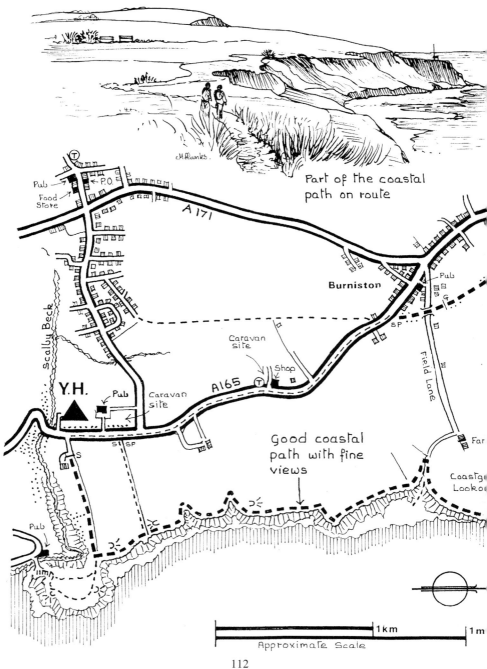

Part of the coastal path on route

M Planks.

Pub
Food Store
P.O.
A 171
Scalby Beck
Burniston
Pub
SP
Field Lane
Caravan site
Shop
Y.H.
Pub
Caravan site
A165
Good coastal path with fine views
Coastg'd Lookou
Far
S
SP
Pub

1km
1m
Approximate Scale

Map 41
Walks around Scarborough YH:
Scarborough to Hayburn Wyke

see page 101

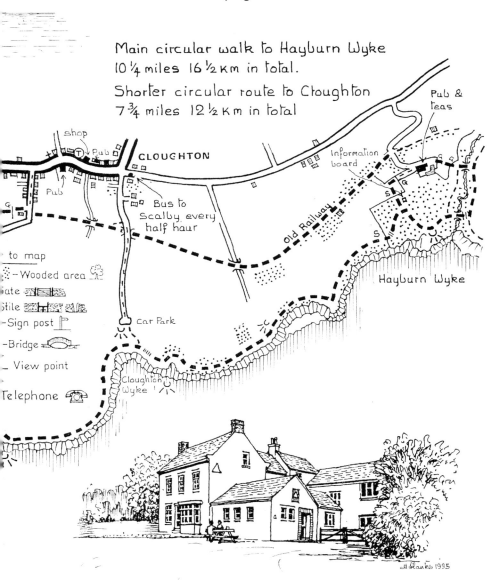

Main circular walk to Hayburn Wyke
10¼ miles 16½ Km in total.

Shorter circular route to Cloughton
7¾ miles 12½ Km in total

Pub &
teas

shop
Pub
CLOUGHTON

Information
board

Pub

Bus to
Scalby every
half hour

Old Railway

Hayburn Wyke

to map
— Wooded area
ate
Stile
—Sign post
—Bridge
_ View point

Telephone

Car Park

Cloughton
Wyke

M. Planks 1995

Scarborough Youth Hostel Tel- 01723-361176

Slaidburn Youth Hostel

Map 42 (see page 116/117)

Slaidburn to Dunsop Bridge   11 miles (17.5km)

This walk takes you down the valley of the River Hodder, past Newton to reach Dunsop Bridge, where you can picnic by the bridge. From here, a path cuts through fields and belts of trees running directly back to Slaidburn. Note the other paths on the map which give a variety of alternatives including a short walk from Slaidburn to Newton, returning via Pain Hill Farm. This route is 4.5 miles (7km) long.

Map 43 (see page 118/119)

Slaidburn to Stocks Reservoir   5 miles (8km)

The main walk heads through a couple of fields to join a track past Hammerton Hall. It continues straight on heading for the reservoir, turning right to reach Black House Farm where it goes south east before returning back to Hammerton Hall. Note the extension of this route to the wood at the end of the reservoir. For shorter routes, there are two options; Out via Myttons Farm Craft Shop, returning via Shay House (4 miles/6.5km) and a very short one of 2.25 miles (3.25km) which goes to Bell Sykes Farm.

Stainforth Youth Hostel (OS Outdoor Leisure Map 2)

Map 44 (see page 120/121)

Stainforth to Settle   5.7 miles (9km)

This path commences opposite the Youth Hostel and follows the line of the Settle and Carlisle railway. Look out for the old lime kiln on the way. The path leaves the railway to enter Longcliffe village and then crosses fields for about a mile to reach Settle. The latter is a popular tourist centre; its ancient properties making it very picturesque. The return path is up Ribblesdale, keeping close to the river for much of the way. This map also shows a short circular walk to Catrigg Force, a pretty waterfall to the east of the village.

Map 45 (see page 122/123)

Stainforth to Pen-y-ghent   13 miles (20.7km)

If you fancy a walk to the summit of Pen-y-ghent (at a height of 2,273 feet above sea level) you can either walk from Stainforth and then drop down to Horton-in-Ribblesdale, or for a shorter walk, catch the bus to the latter and walk up from there. The path leaves Stainforth on the Ribble Way and links up with the Pennine Way, returning down Horton Scar Lane. There is a path which leads back down Ribblesdale to Stainforth from Horton-in-Ribblesdale, following the river down to Helwith Bridge. Progress here is impeded by a quarry, but a lane brings you to Little Stainforth. Here another lane drops down to the river. Before crossing the bridge, walk downstream a short distance to view Stainforth Force.

Thixendale Youth Hostel

Map 46 (see page 124/125)

Thixendale to Fridaythorpe   9.5 miles (15km)

The Wolds Way is used to leave Thixendale before turning left (eastwards) to walk to Fridaythorpe. The path then cuts through a few fields to reach Wold House Farm. Beyond here, there is a short stretch of walking on the busy A166. This can be avoided as the map indicates, although the road walking is uninteresting. The route north of the A166 returns to Thixendale on the Wolds Way. Shortly after leaving the A166, the track is overgrown but easy to follow.

Map 47 (see page 126/127)

Thixendale to Wharram Percy   10 miles (16km)

This route may be reduced in length to 7.7 miles (12.5km) by not going to Wharram Le Street.

From Thixendale it goes northwards, on the village side of Raisthorpe Manor. It is about two miles to the remains of Wharram Percy. This village was abandoned about 500 years ago. The church is ruined but the walls and much of the tower remains. The foundations of the houses and paddock boundaries are grassed over but may be seen as a regular pattern on the hillside. This fascinating site is well worth a visit.

From Wharram Percy proceed to Bella Farm — either directly or via Wharram Le Street. The lane is then taken back to the hostel, turning right at the junction.

Map 42   Walks around Slaidburn YH:
Slaidburn to Dunsop Bridge

see page 114

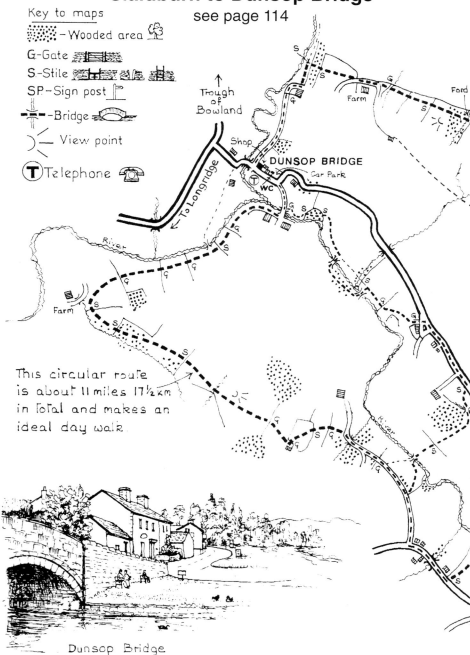

Key to maps

::::: – Wooded area 🌳

G–Gate

S–Stile

SP–Sign post

–Bridge

)– View point

(T) Telephone ☎

↑
Trough
of
Bowland

To Longridge

River

Shop

DUNSOP BRIDGE

Car Park

WC

Farm

Ford

Farm

This circular route
is about 11 miles 17½km
in total and makes an
ideal day walk.

River

Dunsop Bridge

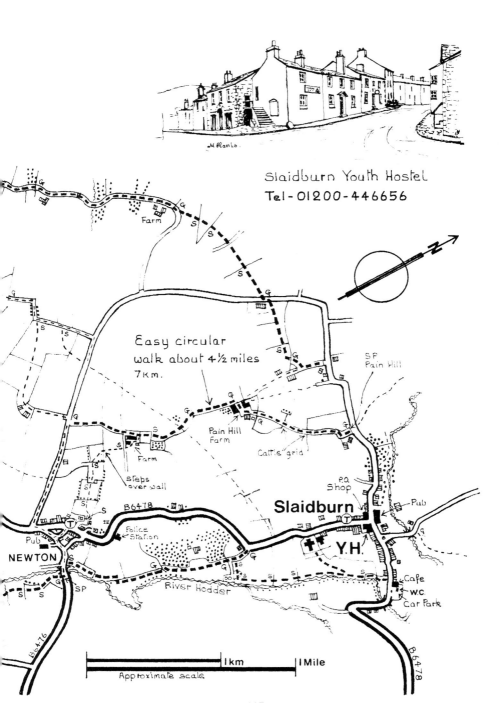

Slaidburn Youth Hostel
Tel- 01200-446656

Easy circular walk about 4½ miles 7 km.

Map 43   Walks around Slaidburn YH:
Slaidburn to Stocks Reservoir
see page 114

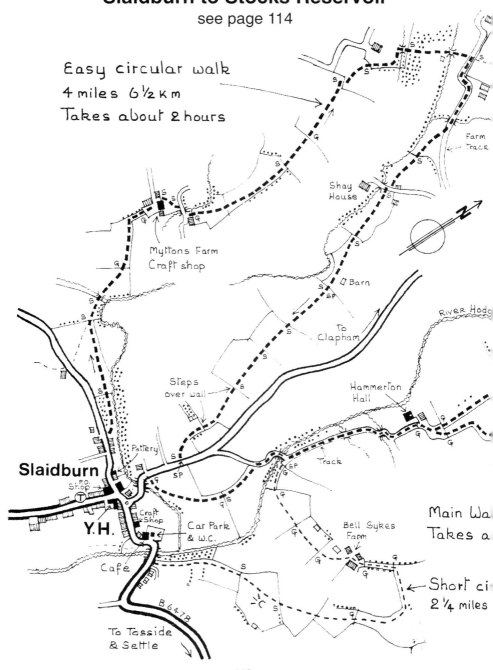

Easy circular walk
4 miles 6½ km
Takes about 2 hours

Farm Track

Shay House

Myttons Farm Craft shop

River Hodd

Barn

To Clapham

Steps over wall

Hammerton Hall

Slaidburn

P.O. Shop

Pottery

Track

Y.H.

Craft Shop

Car Park & W.C.

Bell Sykes Farm

Main Wa

Takes a

Cafe

Short ci
2¼ miles

B 6478

To Tosside & Settle

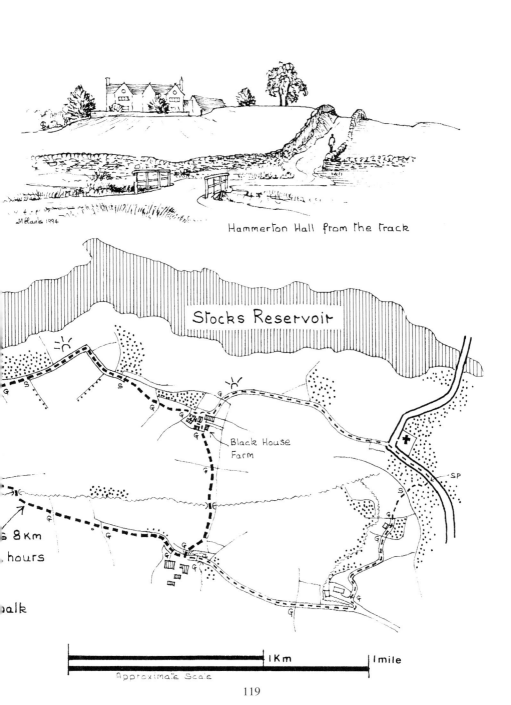

Hammerton Hall from the track

Stocks Reservoir

Black House Farm

8 km

hours

alk

1 Km   1 mile

Approximate Scale

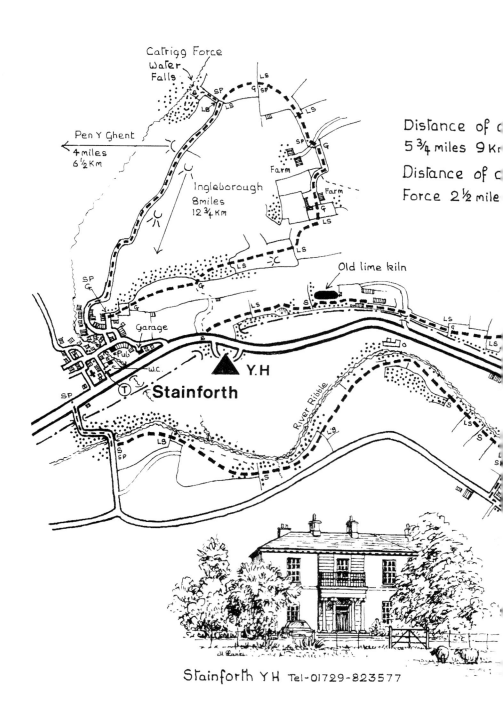

Catrigg Force Water Falls

LS
SP
G SP
LS
LB
LS

Pen Y Ghent
← 4 miles
6½ Km

SP
G

Farm

Ingleborough
8 miles
12¾ Km

Farm
G
LS

Distance of c
5¾ miles 9 Kr

Distance of c
Force 2½ mile

SP
G

Old lime kiln

LS
G
LS

Garage

Pub

W.C.

▲ Y.H

Stainforth

SP

River Ribble

LB
SP

LS

Stainforth Y H Tel-01729-823577

120

Map 44   Walks around Stainforth YH:
Stainforth to Settle

see page 114

...alk to Settle

...alk to Catrigg
...oral.

The Market Place Settle

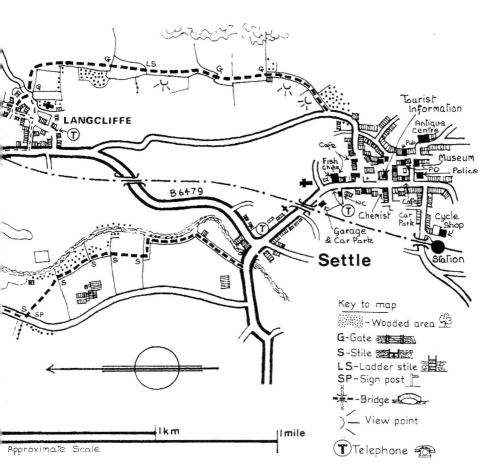

LANGCLIFFE

Tourist Information

Antique Centre

Pub

Cafe

Fish Chips

Museum

PO   Police

B 6479

WC

Cafe

Chemist   Car Park

Cycle Shop

Garage & Car Park

Settle

Station

Key to map

▓▓ – Wooded area 🌳

G – Gate

S – Stile

LS – Ladder stile

SP – Sign post

–▪– – Bridge

)⌒ – View point

ⓣ Telephone ☎

1 km   1 mile

Approximate Scale

121

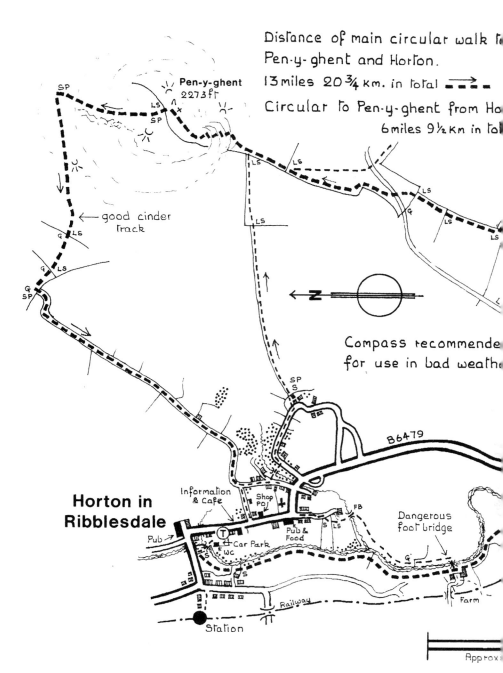

Distance of main circular walk f[...]
Pen-y-ghent and Horton.

13 miles 20¾ km. in total ▪▪▪➤▪▪

Circular to Pen-y-ghent from Ho[...]
6 miles 9½ km in to[...]

Compass recommende[...]
for use in bad weath[...]

Pen-y-ghent
2273 ft

← good cinder track

Horton in
Ribblesdale

Information
& Cafe

Shop
PO

Pub →

Car Park

WC

B6479

Dangerous
foot bridge

Pub &
Food

FB

Railway

Station

Farm

Approx[...]

122

Map 45   Walks around Stainforth YH:
Stainforth to Pen-y-ghent
see page 115

Pen-y-ghent from Horton church

Recommended
direction to walk

Stainforth

Y.H.

Bus stop &
Shelter

Pub

River Ribble

Helwith Br

Moor Head Lane

Bus times from Stainforth to Horton
Mon to Fri 0835. 0950. 1210
Sat 1050. 1250
Return - Horton to Stainforth
Mon to Fri 1540. 1550. 1735. 1740
Sat   1305. 1505. 1705.
Check these times with warden

1km   1mile

Map 46
Walks around Thixendale YH:
Thixendale to Fridaythorpe
see page 115

Thixendale Youth Hostel
Tel – 01377-288230.

Pub

Cafe & shop
Butcher

Interesting little
church

Part of Wolds Way on route

1 km

Approximate Scale

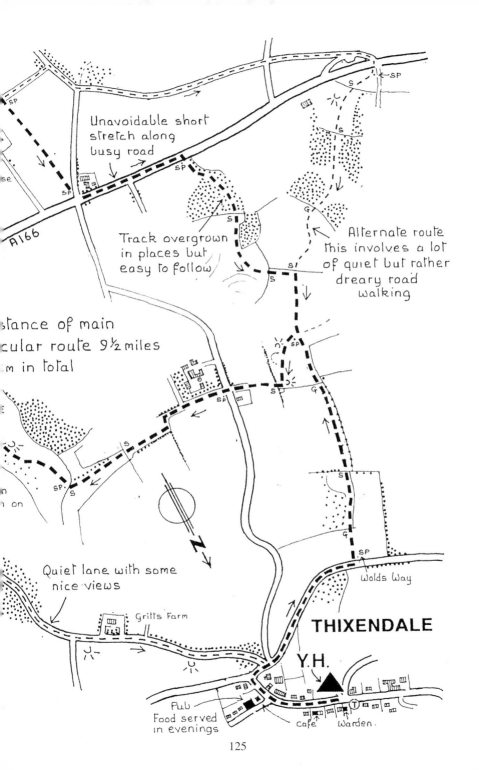

Unavoidable short stretch along busy road

SP

A166

Track overgrown in places but easy to follow

Alternate route this involves a lot of quiet but rather dreary road walking

stance of main cular route 9½ miles m in total

on

Quiet lane with some nice views

Gritts Farm

Wolds Way

THIXENDALE

Y.H.

Pub
Food served in evenings

Cafe   Warden.

Map 47   Walks around Thixendale YH:
Thixendale to Wharram Percy
see page 115

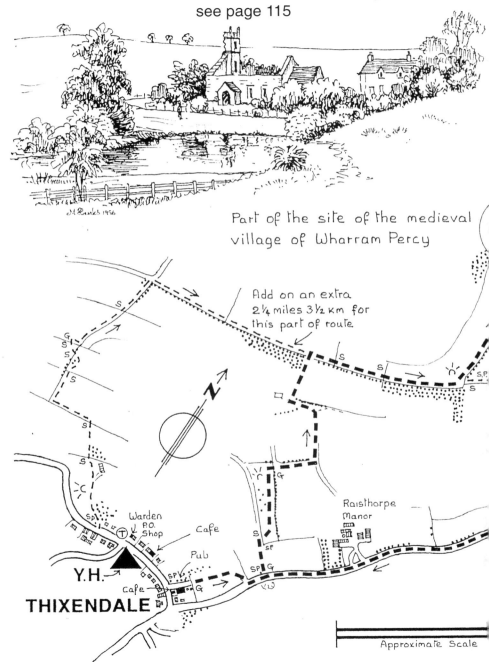

Part of the site of the medieval
village of Wharram Percy

Add on an extra
2¼ miles 3½ km for
this part of route

Raisthorpe Manor

Warden P.O. Shop

Cafe

Pub

Y.H.

Cafe

THIXENDALE

Approximate Scale

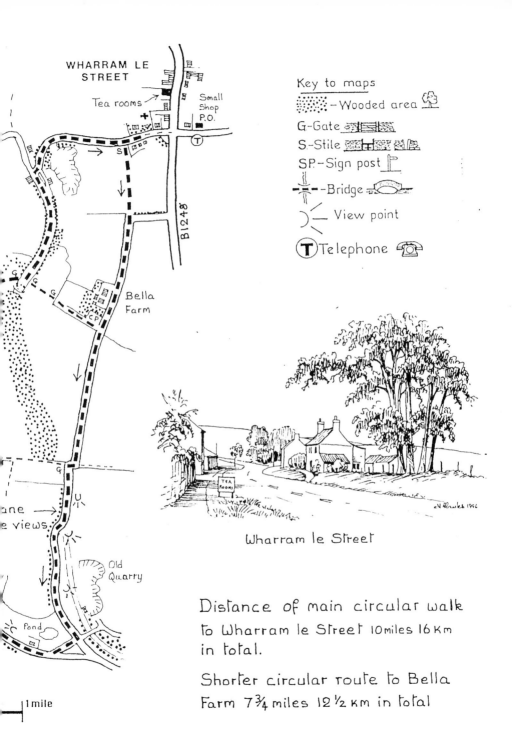

Key to maps

∴∴∴ – Wooded area 🌳

G – Gate

S – Stile

SP – Sign post

━╪━ – Bridge

🌙 – View point

Ⓣ Telephone ☎

WHARRAM LE STREET

Tea rooms

Small Shop P.O.

B1248

Bella Farm

ane
e views.

Old Quarry

Pond

1 mile

Wharram le Street

Distance of main circular walk to Wharram le Street 10 miles 16 Km in total.

Shorter circular route to Bella Farm 7¾ miles 12½ Km in total

127

Wheeldale Youth Hostel

Map 48 (see page 130/131)

Wheeldale to Saltergate   9 miles (14.5km)

The route follows the path to the Blawath Beck and then through Cropton Forest to reach Newtondale Halt on the North Yorkshire Moors Railway. From here a path climbs up to the Saltergate Inn on the A169. It returns to Newton Dale and takes a more northerly path to return to Wheeldale.

An alternative route is available if you can fit in with the train timetable and take the steam train from Newtondale Halt to Goathland Station and alight there, returning by lanes to Wheeldale (described below).

Map 49 (see page 132/133)

Wheeldale to Goathland   9 miles (14.5km)

From the youth hostel, descend to and cross the Wheeldale Beck to reach the Roman road. The route heads northwest, crossing the Wheeldale Beck again and then heading to Hazel Head before descending to cross the West Beck by a footbridge near to the road. Here the path follows the beck up through Scar Wood before climbing out into Goathland village. There is a short circular walk from here to Beck Hole village. It takes in a good view down to the steam railway line before following the general line of the railway via Darnholm to Beck Hole. The pub here is claimed to be one of the smallest in England.

The preferred route runs directly back to Goathland although a route is shown on the map via the West Beck. A minor road runs back to the youth hostel via the Mallyan Hotel on the outskirts of Goathland.

Whitby Youth Hostel

Maps 50 & 51 (see pages 134/135 & 136/137)

Whitby to Stainsacre and Ruswarp   7.5 miles (12km)

Take the cliff path southwards to the lighthouse before heading inland along tracks, lanes and through fields to Stainsacre. Here the path heads westwards to Cock Mill Wood before crossing Rigg Mill Beck. The path returns to the beck at Golden Grove and heads through woodland towards the River Esk, which is crossed at Ruswarp village. Return to Whitby down the side of the river. Try and keep some time spare to visit Whitby Abbey ruins (behind the youth hostel) and Captain Cook's House, now a museum.

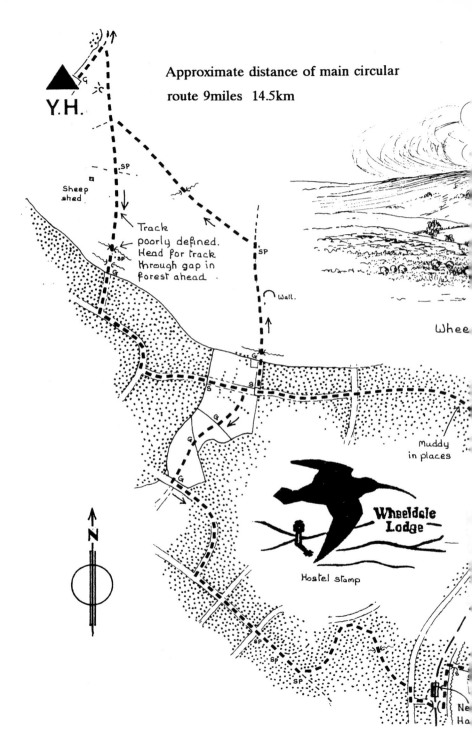

Y.H.

Approximate distance of main circular
route 9miles 14.5km

SP

Sheep
shed

Track
poorly defined.
Head for track
through gap in
forest ahead.

SP

Wall.

Whee

Muddy
in places

N

Wheeldale
Lodge

Hostel stamp

Ne
Ha

Map 48
Walks around Wheeldale YH:
Wheeldale to Saltergate
see page 128

see page 128

Key to maps

▒▒ - Wooded area 🌳
G - Gate 🚧
S. - Stile 🪜
S.P. - Sign post 🪧
╬ - Bridge 🌉
)⌒(View point
(T) Telephone ☎

Hostel
Tel: 01947·896350

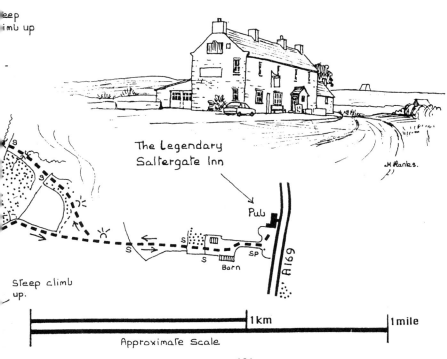

eep
imb up

The Legendary
Saltergate Inn

M Ranks.

Pub

S

S

SP

Barn

A169

Steep climb
up.

| 1km   1 mile
Approximate Scale

Map 49   Walks around Wheeldale YH:
Wheeldale to Goathland

see page 128

Approximate distance of main circular

route 9miles   14.5km

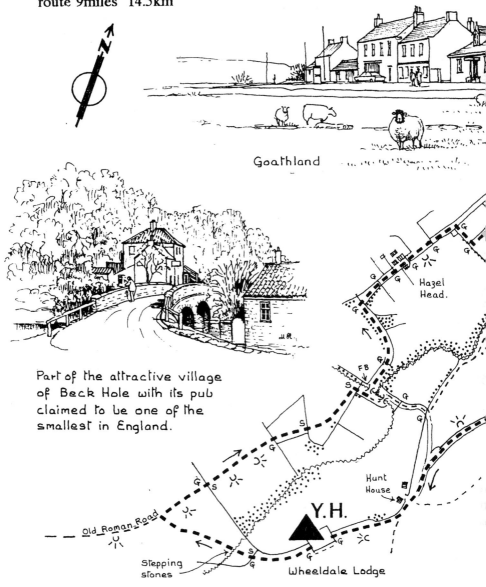

Goathland

Part of the attractive village
of Beck Hole with its pub
claimed to be one of the
smallest in England.

Hazel
Head.

FB

Hunt
House

Y.H.

Old Roman Road

Stepping
Stones

Wheeldale Lodge

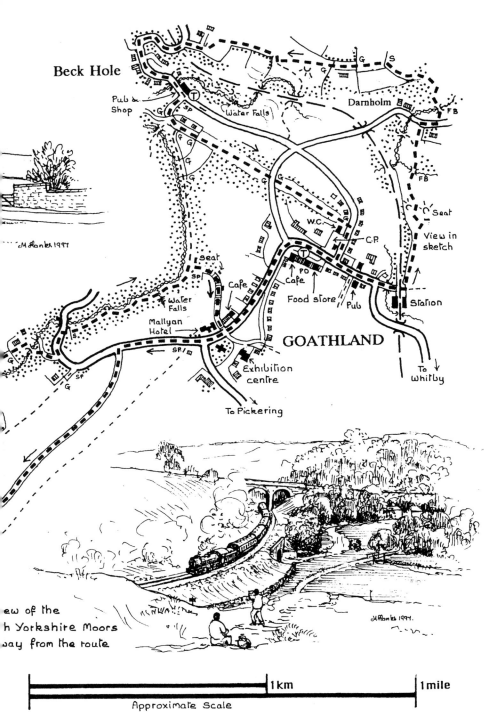

Beck Hole

Pub & Shop

Water Falls

Darnholm

FB

FB

Seat

View in sketch

W.C.

C.P.

Seat

Cafe

PO
Cafe

Food store

Pub

Station

Water Falls

Mallyan Hotel

GOATHLAND

Exhibition centre

To Pickering

To Whitby

M.Banks 1997

ew of the
h Yorkshire Moors
ay from the route

M.Banks 1994.

| 1km | 1 mile |

Approximate Scale

Map 50
Walks around Whitby YH:
Whitby Town
see page 128

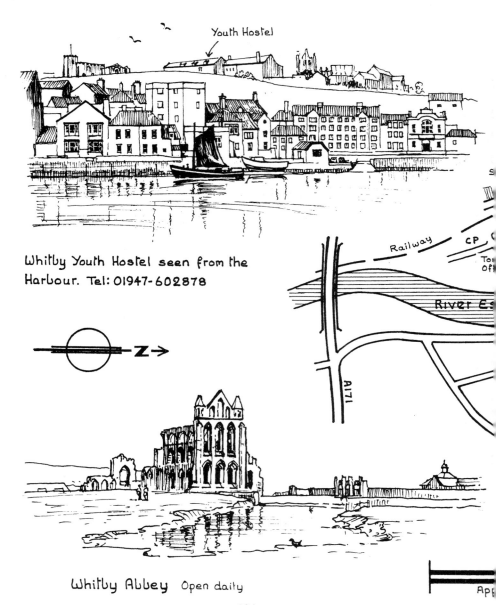

Youth Hostel

Whitby Youth Hostel seen from the
Harbour. Tel: 01947-602878

Railway   CP

River E

A171

Whitby Abbey Open daily

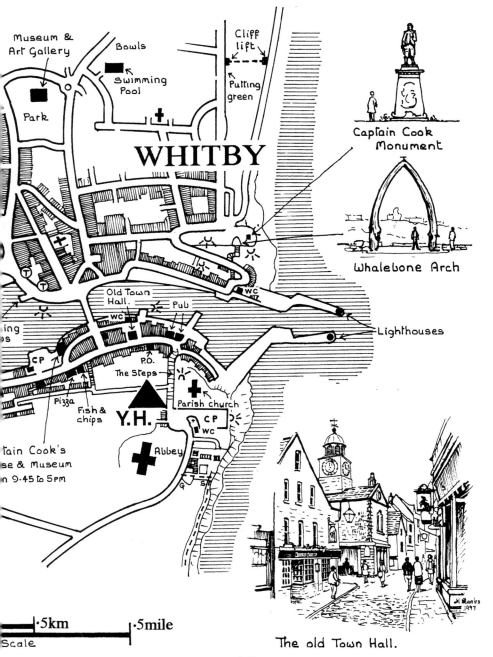

Museum &
Art Gallery

Bowls

Cliff
lift

Putting
green

Swimming
Pool

Park

WHITBY

Captain Cook
Monument

Whalebone Arch

Old Town
Hall.

Pub

WC

WC

Lighthouses

CP

...ing
...s

P.O.

The Steps

Pizza

Fish &
chips

Y.H.

Parish church

CP
WC

...tain Cook's
...se & Museum
...n 9·45 to 5pm

Abbey

·5km   ·5mile

Scale

The old Town Hall.

135

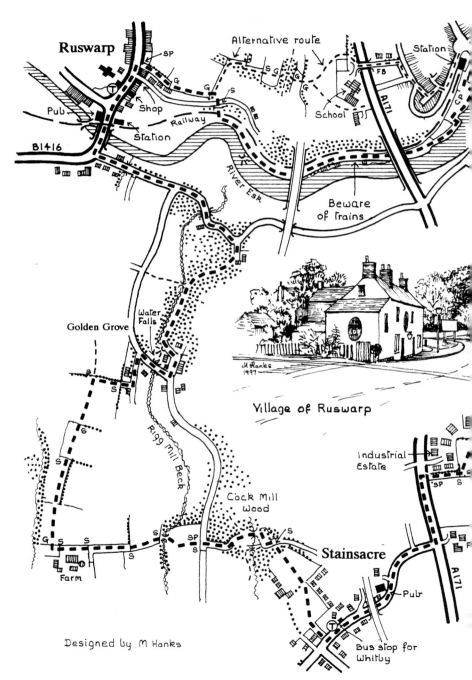

Ruswarp

SP

Alternative route

Station

SG

G   G

G

S   G

FB

A171

Pub

Shop

Station

Railway

School

B1416

River Esk

Beware
of Trains

Water
Falls

Golden Grove

Village of Ruswarp

M Hanks
1997

Rigg Mill Beck

S   G

S

Industrial
Estate

SP   S

Cock Mill
Wood

S

S

Stainsacre

G   S   S

S

SP

S

S

F

Farm

Pub

A171

Designed by M Hanks

T

Bus stop for
Whitby

Map 51   Walks around Whitby YH:
Whitby to Stainsacre and Ruswarp
see page 128

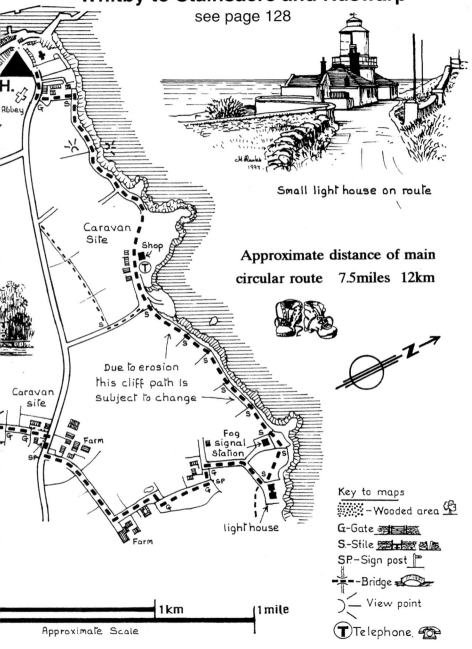

Small light house on route

Approximate distance of main
circular route   7.5miles 12km

H. +

Abbey

Caravan Site

Shop

Caravan site

Due to erosion
this cliff path is
subject to change

Farm

Fog
signal
Station

SP

Farm

light house

Key to maps

- Wooded area
- G-Gate
- S.-Stile
- SP.-Sign post
- Bridge
- View point
- (T) Telephone.

1km   1mile

Approximate Scale

INTER HOSTEL WALKING ROUTES

Upper Dales Four Hostels Walk (OS Outdoor Leisure Map 30)

Area Map 52 (see page 140/141)

Map 53 (see pages 142/143 and 144/145)

Aysgarth YH to Grinton YH   12 miles (19km)

This route follows the path to Castle Bolton (described under walks around Aysgarth) with a minor alternative route into Castle Bolton, where there is a cafe in the castle.

The path climbs up onto Bolton Moor to the shooting shelter here (marked on the map). The main route goes to the north west from here across East Bolton Moor, but if required, there is a direct path to Grinton from Dent House.

The track across East Bolton Moor (Apedale Road) is an old miner's track. There are many shafts, levels and shake holes (cave systems) in this area which should be avoided. Upon reaching Swaledale, the path runs parallel to the valley along Harkerside Moor before dropping down into Grinton.

Map 54 (see pages 146/147 and 148/149)

Grinton YH to Keld YH   15 miles (24km)

The path starts by descending into Swaledale to cross Grinton Bridge and then Reeth Bridge over the River Swale and the Arkle Beck respectively. A track is taken to Healaugh through the fields close to the River Swale. Having proceeded through the village it then heads for Surrender Bridge. The path proceeds through the Barney Beck at the edge of Birkpark Wood with views down towards the beck. The path soon reaches moorland which has been heavily worked in the past for lead ore. The Old Gang Mine in this valley was particularly well known in times gone by as a productive mine. There are remains of old smelting mills in the valley where the ore was reduced to ingots of metal. The path follows an old mine track up to the upper reaches of the valley or beck. It then heads westwards across Melbecks Moor on a walled track before descending into Gunnerside Gill. There is a choice of two descents into the valley but both are rather steep.

From the Lownathwaite Mine the path continues in a generally westerly direction across Gunnerside Moor. Much of this is on a good track heading for the old Swinner Gill lead mines. Look out for the waterfalls in this area before you cross Swinner Gill and then proceed past Crackpot Hall, Kisdon Force and East Gill Force before you cross the River Swale to reach Keld.

Note that there are no refreshments available between Reeth and Keld.

Map 55 (see pages 150/151 and 152/153)

Keld YH to Hawes YH

15 miles (24km)

This route follows the Pennine Way for much of the day, heading generally in a southerly direction with a climb over Great Shunner Fell before dropping down to the River Ure and Hawes.

Leaving the hostel along the B6270 take the path which heads for Muker described in the walks around Keld section above. However, having reached Kisdon Farm bear westwards to descend into Thwaite on the Pennine Way. Follow the Pennine Way for a little over 3 miles to reach the summit of Great Shunner Fell. Thereafter the path descends along a ridge to Hardraw and Wensleydale. It then crosses the Ure Valley to reach Hawes. Do not worry about visiting Hardraw Force if time is pressing, the opportunity presents itself if you intend to continue on from Hawes to Aysgarth Falls YH.

Map 56 (see pages 154/155 and 156/157)

Hawes YH to Aysgarth Falls YH

13 miles (21km)

From Hawes village, proceed over the River Ure at Haylands Bridge and walk to Hardraw and then Sedbusk. If you have already seen Hardraw Force from the latter the path goes down Wensleydale passing the farm at Litherskew and Shore Cote before crossing Skel Gill Beck. Beyond here it follows Skelgill Lane before returning to the fields to reach Askrigg. On leaving Askrigg the route heads for the river and then follows the riverbank to Nappa Mill. It then follows the line of the abandoned railway eventually crossing the river just outside Aysgarth. After following the south-side of the river for a short distance to Aysgarth Mill, walk through the fields into the village and then take the path to the church which is just below the youth hostel.

Map 52
Upper Dales Four Hostels Walk

A 55 miles (88km) walk through
the beautiful Yorkshire Dales
connecting four Youth Hostels

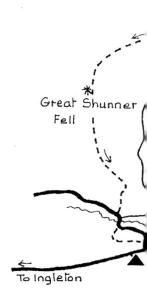

Great Shunner Fell

To Ingleton

Village of Keld

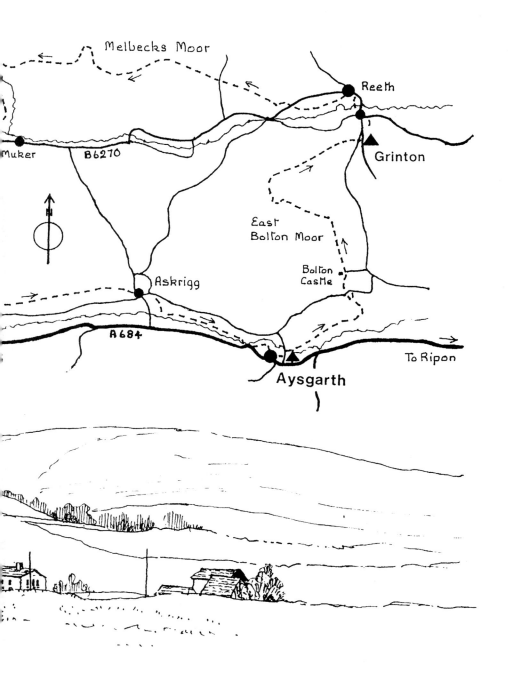

Melbecks Moor

Muker

B6270

Reeth

Grinton

East
Bolton Moor

Bolton
Castle

Askrigg

A684

To Ripon

Aysgarth

Map 53

Aysgarth YH to Grinton YH: part 1
see page 138

Aysgarth to Grinton 12 miles 19 km

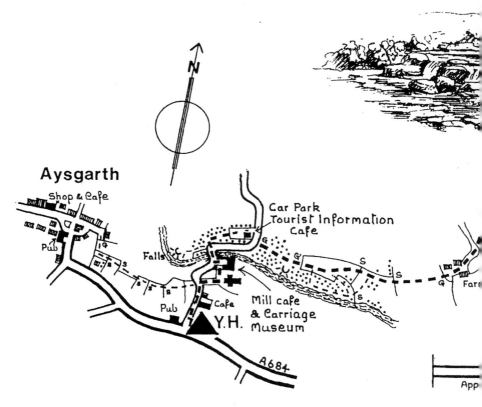

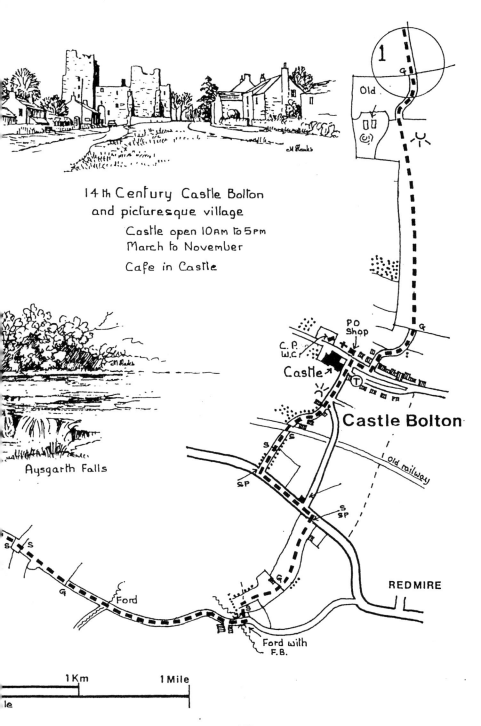

14th Century Castle Bolton
and picturesque village

Castle open 10am to 5pm
March to November

Cafe in Castle

Aysgarth Falls

Castle

Castle Bolton

Old railway

REDMIRE

Ford

Ford with
F.B.

1 Km   1 Mile

Map 53
Aysgarth YH to Grinton YH: part 2

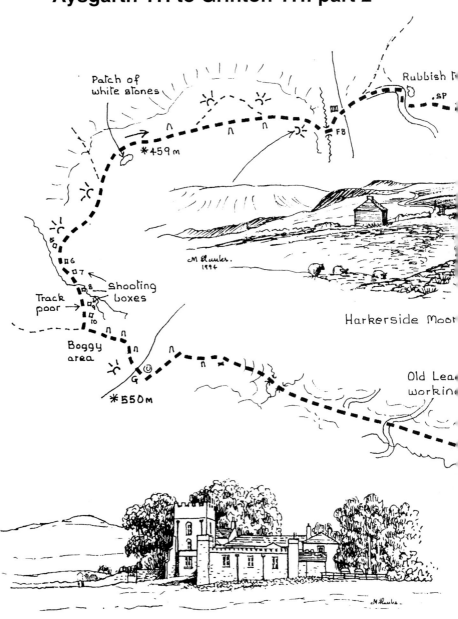

Patch of white stones

Rubbish I

.SP

F8

*459m

M. Hawles.
1996

Harkerside Moor

5
6
7
Shooting boxes
Track poor
8
9
10

Boggy area

G

Old Lea working

*550m

Grinton Lodge Youth Hostel
Tel 01748-884206

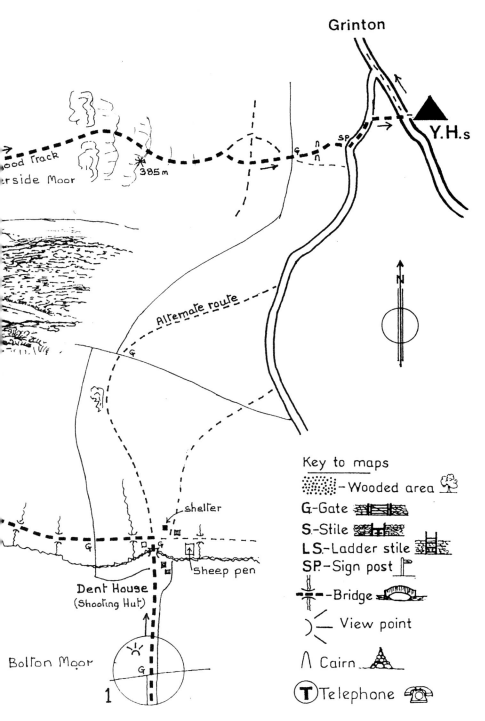

Grinton

Y.H.s

ood Track
rside Moor

385 m

Alternate route

N

Key to maps

- Wooded area
G-Gate
S.-Stile
L.S.-Ladder stile
S.P.-Sign post
-Bridge
) View point
Λ Cairn
T Telephone

shelter

Sheep pen

Dent House
(Shooting Hut)

Bolton Moor

1

145

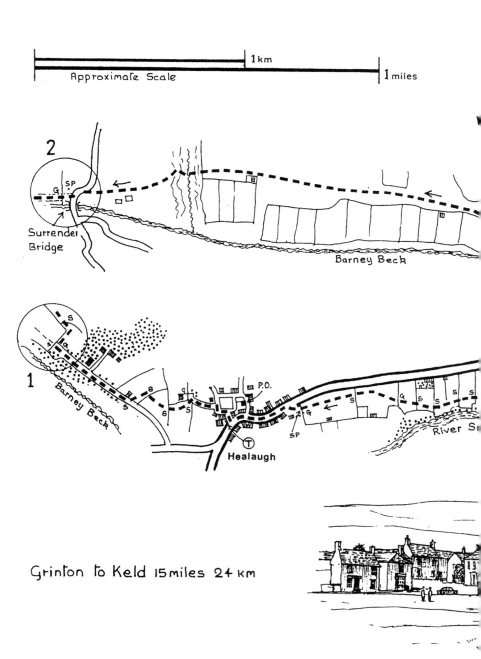

2

SP

G

Surrender
Bridge

Barney Beck

1

Barney Beck

S

P.O.

Healaugh

SP

G

River S

Grinton to Keld 15 miles 24 km

1 km
Approximate Scale
1 miles

Map 54
Grinton YH to Keld YH: part 1
see page 138

St Andrews Grinton

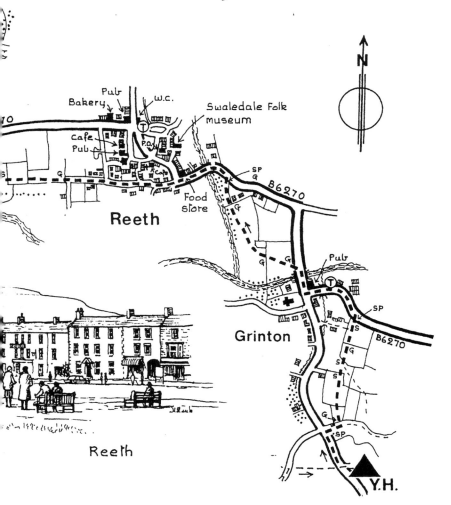

N

Pub
Bakery
W.C.
Swaledale Folk
museum
Cafe
P.O.
Pub
Cafe
SP
B6270
Food
store
Reeth
Pub
SP
Grinton
B6270

Reeth

Y.H.

Map 54
Grinton YH to Keld YH: part 2

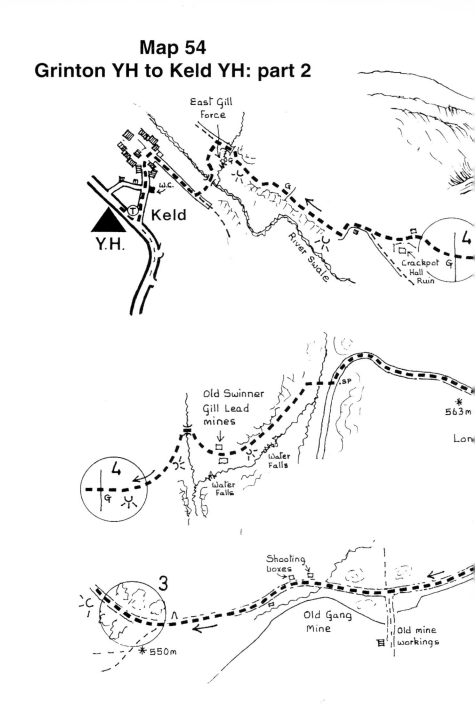

East Gill Force

Keld

Y.H.

River Swale

Crackpot Hall Ruin

W.C.

4

Old Swinner Gill Lead mines

Water Falls

Water Falls

.SP

563m

Lon

4

3

Shooting boxes

Old Gang Mine

Old mine workings

*550m

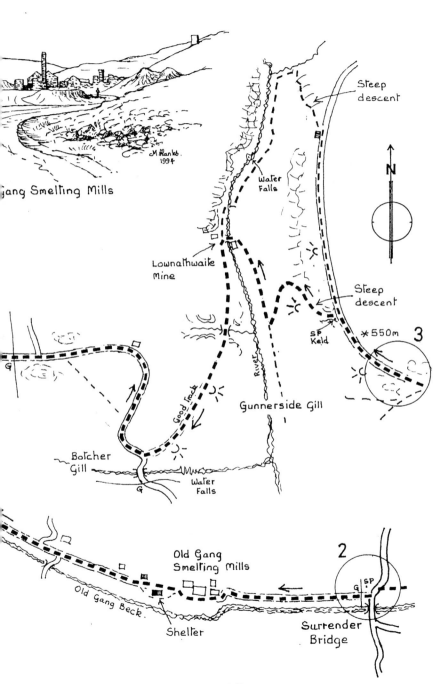

Steep descent

M. Planks. 1994

...ang Smelting Mills

Water Falls

N

Lownathwaite Mine

Steep descent

Steep descent

SP Keld

*550m

3

River

Good Track

Gunnerside Gill

Botcher Gill

G

Water Falls

Old Gang Smelting Mills

2

Old Gang Beck.

SP
G

Shelter

Surrender Bridge

Map 55

Keld YH to Hawes YH: part 1
see page 139

Keld to Hawes 15 miles 24 km.

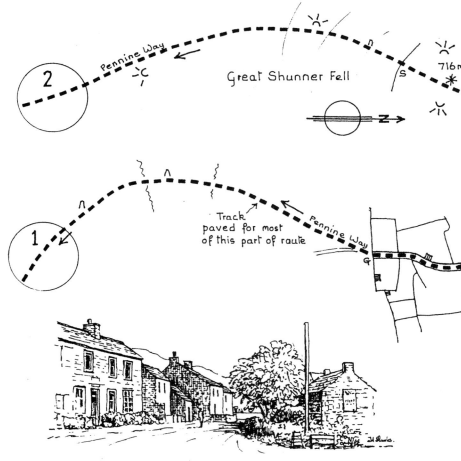

Pennine Way

2

C

Great Shunner Fell

716 m

S

N

Z

1

Track
paved for most
of this part of route

Pennine Way

G

Village of Thwaite

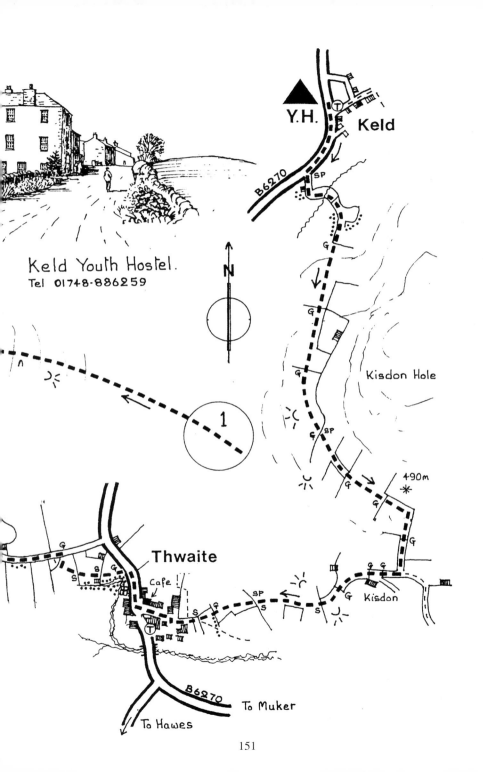

Y.H.

Keld

B6270

SP

Kisdon Hole

Keld Youth Hostel.
Tel 01748-886259

N

(1)

490m

Thwaite

Cafe

Kisdon

B6270

To Muker

To Hawes

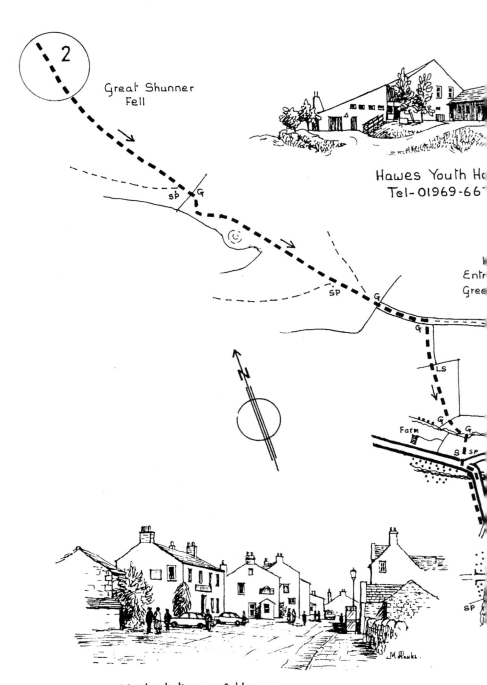

2

Great Shunner
Fell

SP G

SP G

G

LS

Farm

G G

S SP

Hawes Youth H...
Tel- 01969-66...

Entr...
Gree...

SP

Market Town of Hawes

M. Hawes.

152

Map 55
Keld YH to Hawes YH: part 2

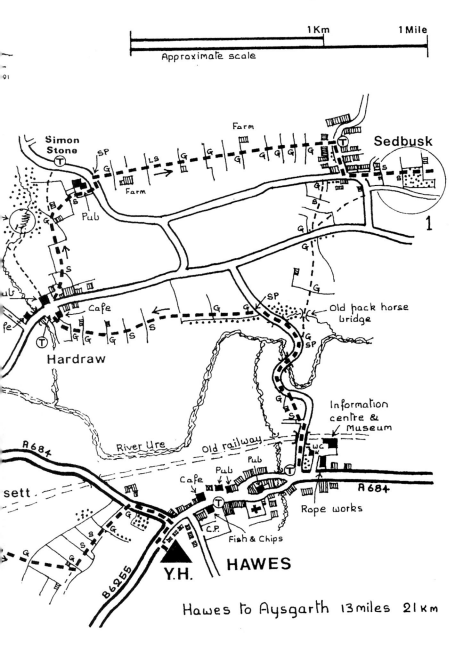

HAWES

Y.H.

Hawes to Aysgarth 13 miles 21 km

Map 56

Hawes YH to Aysgarth YH: part 1
see page 139

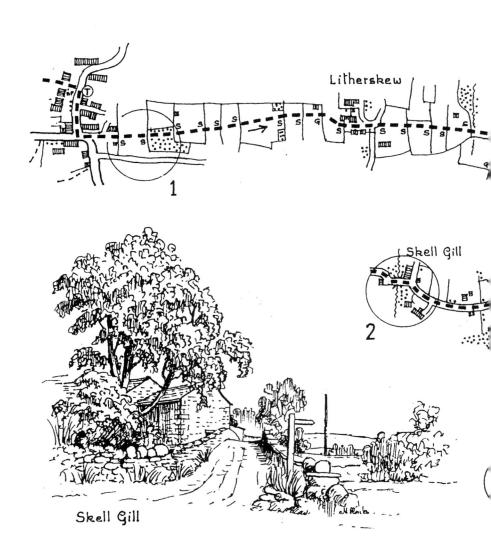

Litherskew

1

Skell Gill

2

Skell Gill

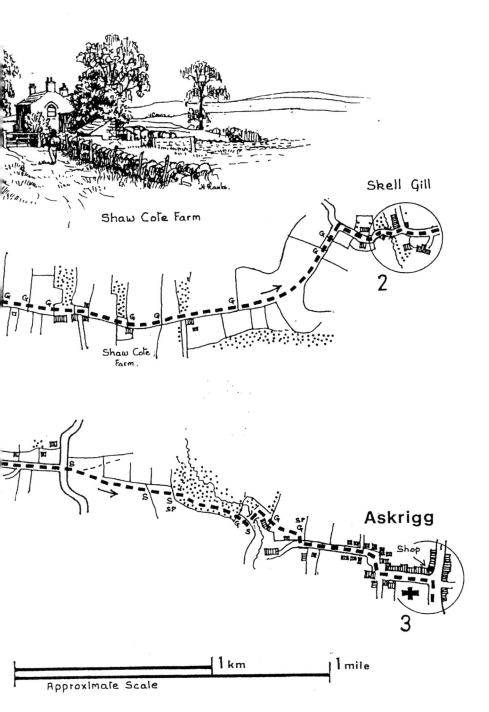

Shaw Cote Farm

Skell Gill

Shaw Cote Farm.

2

Askrigg

Shop

3

1 km   1 mile

Approximate Scale

Map 56
Hawes YH to Aysgarth YH: part 2

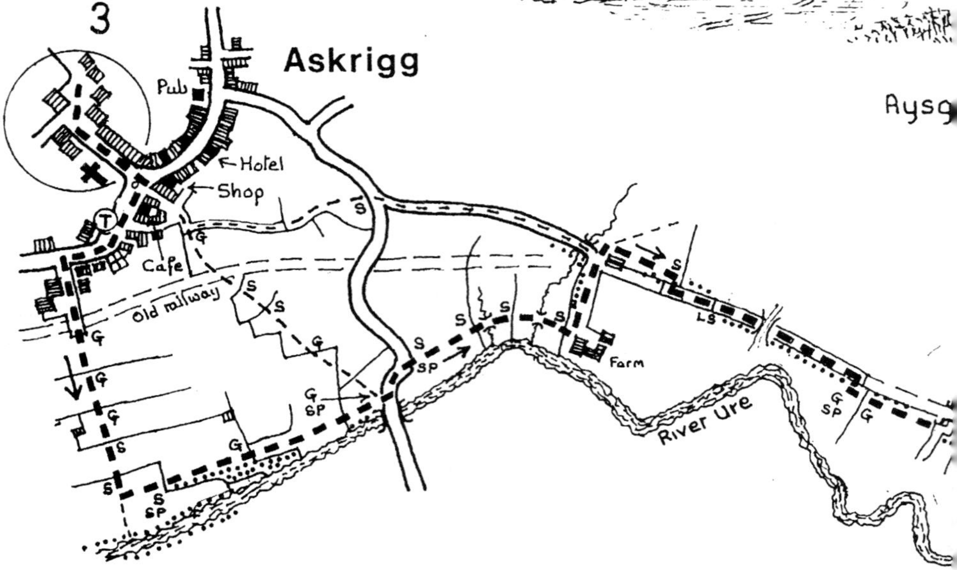

M Hanks.

3

Askrigg

Aysg

Pub

Hotel

Shop

T

Cafe

Old railway

Farm

River Ure

Askrigg Church

It is recommended that the Ordnance Survey Map 1-25,000 is also used when making this walk.

Village

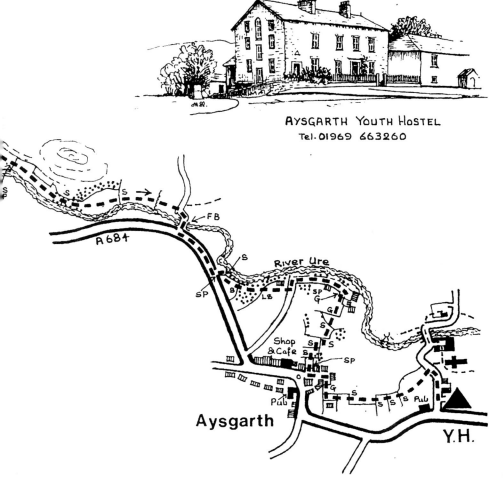

AYSGARTH YOUTH HOSTEL
Tel. 01969 663260

157

Lower Dales 3 Hostels Walk (OS Outdoor Leisure Maps 2 & 30)

Area Map 57 (see page 160/161)

Map 58 (see pages 162/163 and 164/165)

Kettlewell YH to Linton YH   11 miles (17.5km)

This route follows the Dales Way between Kettlewell and Grassington. It commences by walking through a series of small fields which preserve some of the ancient strip boundaries of the former open field system of Kettlewell. After a mile or so the route then climbs out of Wharfedale up onto the moorland area above. The path passes through fine open moorland with good views. After about 3 miles the Dales Way drops down towards Grassington. Beyond Grassington the path follows the River Wharfe for about a mile before crossing the river and heading across fields to the B6160. A lane continues into Thorpe. Just beyond the village a path cuts across to Linton emerging in the latter close to the youth hostel.

Map 59 (see pages 166/167 and 168/169)

Linton YH to Malham YH   10 miles (16km)

From Linton the route heads across the fields and the B6265 to reach Skirethorns. After walking through the village the road is left for Wood Nook Caravan Site heading for the ruins of Height Laithe Farm. The route starts to climb up onto the moors and continues on past the hamlet of Bordley where it heads north to join Mastiles Lane. This is an old unpaved drover's road crossing the moors. At this point it is possible to branch off and head straight to Malham which is useful if the weather is poor. It proceeds down Hawthorns Lane via Lee Gate Farm. Before entering Malham you can visit Janet's Foss below the road to your left. Otherwise continue along Mastiles Lane to Malham Tarn and then head south for Malham via Malham Cove. The last two miles is undoubtedly the most interesting of this day's route and ends with a spectacular descent into Malham Cove.

Map 60 (see pages 170/171 and 172/173)

Malham YH to Kettlewell YH   11 miles (17.5km)

Given good weather this a full days walk with impressive scenery along the whole of the route. It proceeds to Malham Tarn via Gordale Scar. This route is described in the walks around Malham section above. From Malham Tarn the route takes the Monk's Road and crosses some fine open moorland before descending into the attractive village of Arncliffe, where a pub and cafe can be found. From here a path climbs back up onto the moors before a scenic descent into Wharfedale and Kettlewell.

Boggle Hole YH to Wheeldale YH   15 miles (24km)

Maps 61 & 62 (see pages 174/175 and 176/177)

Note that there is no where to obtain refreshments on the main route. The latter leaves the coast, climbing up towards Fylingdales Moor via Browside Farm. It crosses the A171 Whitby to Scarborough road, a mile south of the Flask Inn. An alternative route comes up to the Flask Inn and then heads south down the A171 to reach the main route.

From here, it is essential that you have a 1:25,000 OS Map for the next stage which crosses Fylingdales Moor, heading for the Cross on Lilla Howe, just north of Burn Howe Rigg at 3116 feet (959m) above sea level.

The path then follows a stream to reach the A169, the Whitby – Pickering road before dropping down to cross the North Yorkshire Moors Railway. From here, it's another three miles of open moorland to reach Wheeldale youth hostel. This route shoud not be attempted unless you are an experienced walker, well kitted out and not in bad weather.

Scarborough YH to Lockton YH   14.5 miles (23km)

Map 63 (see pages 178/179 and 180/181)

The map shows an alternative route which can be used to return on foot to Scarborough. It involves more road walking than the outward journey and there is also some retracing of ones steps in places. Alternatively, you can either walk from Lockton youth hostel to Pickering, or if operating, catch the steam train to Pickering Station and then catch the bus back to Scarborough from Pickering.

From the hostel turn left on the A156 and then left again to walk to Scalby. Go through the village on the road to Hacknes. Part of this section is on the road but the middle piece cuts through the fields and some belts of woodland. Continue on the road from Hackness towards Broxa. The path bears to the left upon reaching a signpost. Having cut through the woodland, 3 fields are passed before Broxa is reached. A further section of using pathways and the road brings you to Langdale End and then there is a 3 to 4 mile section of road walking through the forest. Hereafter the bulk of the path runs through fields to Lockton.

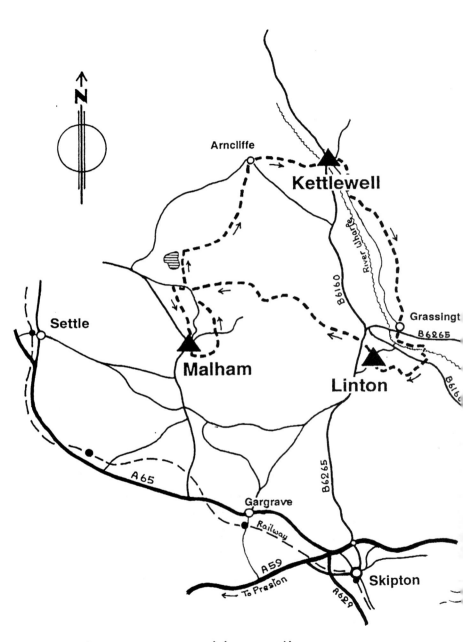

Area covered by walk

Map 57

Lower Dales Three Hostels Walk

This 32 mile (51km) circular route, which is based
on Kettlewell, Linton and Malham Youth Hostels
has been chosen so as to take in some of the finest
scenery in the area.

Although this map has been designed to start and
finish at Kettlewell, the route works equally well
if started at any one of the three hostels.

M Ranks 1996.

Janet's Foss
Waterfall near Malham passed on route

Map 58
Kettlewell YH to Linton YH: part 1
see page 158

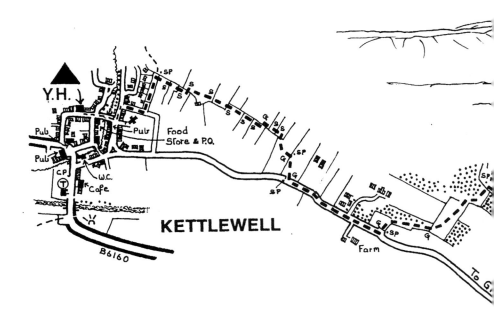

KETTLEWELL

After starting by walking through small fields for the first mile, the route then climbs out of the valley where a stretch of fine open moorland with good views follows until you descend into Grassington. This attractive old town makes an ideal lunch stop as it has plenty of places for refreshment.
From here the route follows a very picturesque stretch of the river Wharfe finishing with a final mile through pleasant farmland and the small hamlet of Thorpe.

Kettlewell >

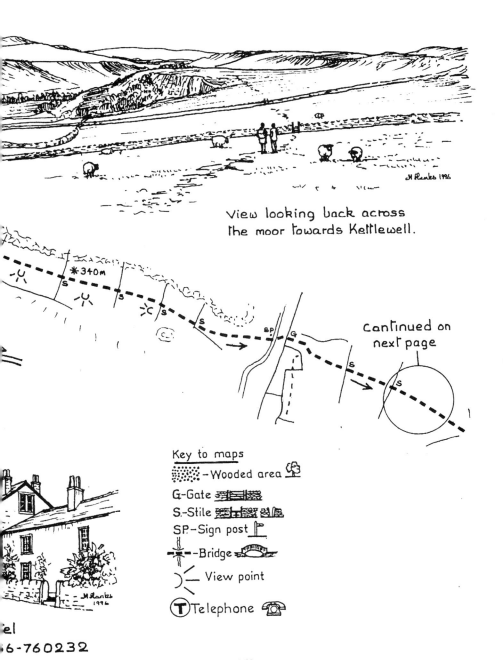

View looking back across the moor towards Kettlewell.

*340m

Continued on next page

Key to maps

▒ – Wooded area

G-Gate

S.-Stile

SP.–Sign post

━┼━ –Bridge

)⊂ – View point

(T) Telephone

el

6-760232

Map 58
Kettlewell YH to Linton YH: part 2

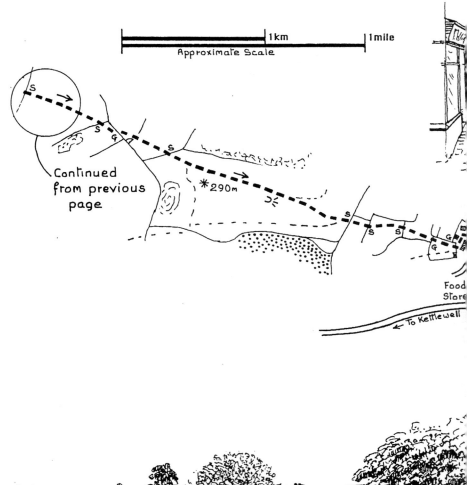

Approximate Scale

1km   1mile

Continued from previous page

*290m

Food Store

To Kettlewell →

M Ranks 1996

Linton Youth Hostel
Tel·01756-752400

Grassington

Cafe

Fish & Chips

Museum

Fish Farm

River Wharfe

National Park Information Centre

WC   CP

B6160

Thorpe

Y.H.

✳ 230m

Farm

Pub

LINTON

Map 59
Linton YH to Malham YH: part 1
see page 158

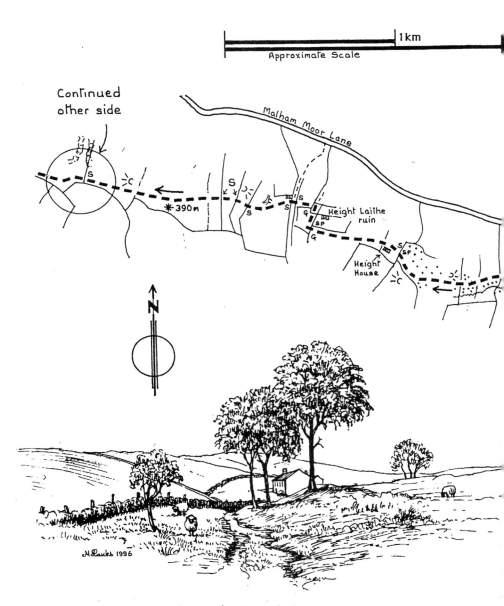

1km

Approximate Scale

Continued
other side

Malham Moor Lane

S

C

* 390m

S

S

S

S

G

SP

Height Laithe
ruin

G

S

SP

Height
House

C

N

View looking towards Height House

M.Hawks 1996

166

The quiet lane heading from
Skirethorns

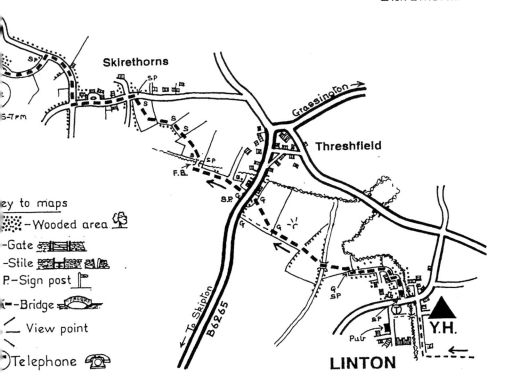

Skirethorns

Threshfield

Grassington →

LINTON

Y.H.

Pub

To Skipton
B6265

ey to maps
- Wooded area
-Gate
-Stile
P.-Sign post
-Bridge
View point
Telephone

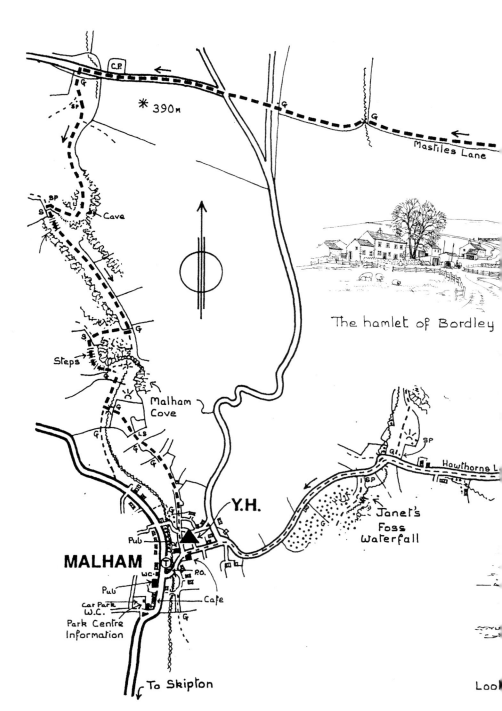

C.P.

* 390m

Mastiles Lane

Cave

SP

S

G

Steps

Malham
Cove

The hamlet of Bordley

Janet's
Foss
Waterfall

Hawthorne L

SP

Y.H.

Pub

MALHAM

W.C.

Pub

Car Park
W.C.

Park Centre
Information

P.O.

Cafe

To Skipton

Lool

Map 59
Linton YH to Malham YH: part 2

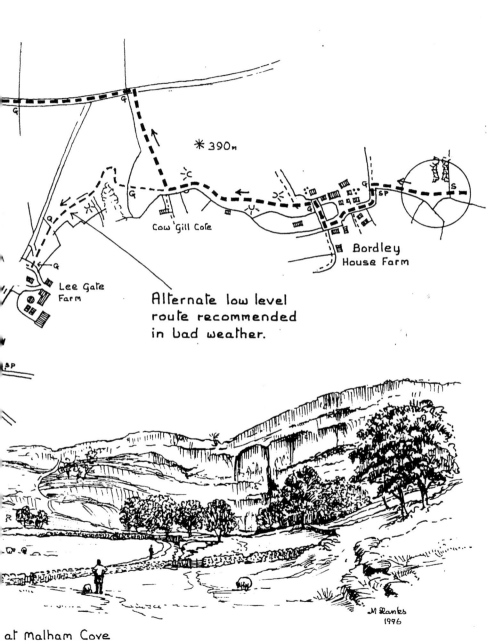

Cow Gill Cote

Bordley
House Farm

Lee Gate
Farm

Alternate low level
route recommended
in bad weather.

* 390m

at Malham Cove

M Ranks
1996

Map 60

Malham YH to Kettlewell YH: part 1
see page 158

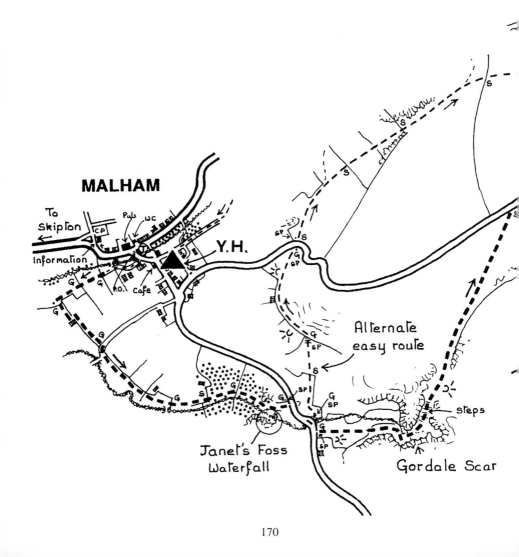

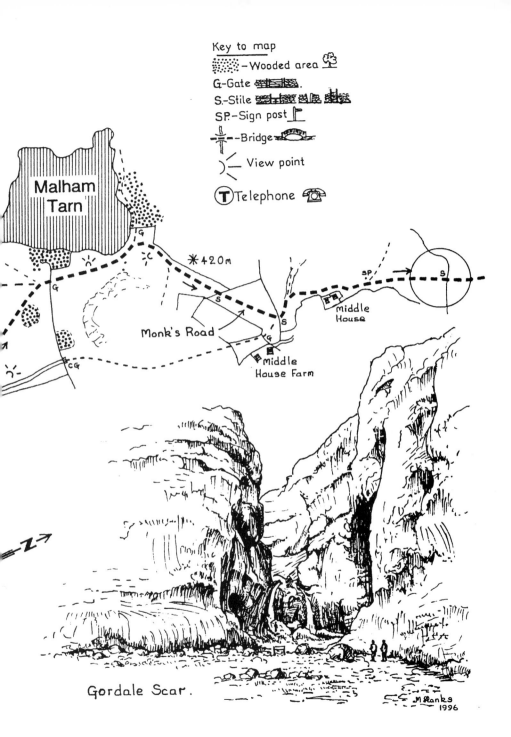

Key to map

- Wooded area
G - Gate
S. - Stile
SP. - Sign post
- Bridge
- View point
(T) Telephone

Malham Tarn

✳ 420m

Monk's Road

Middle House

Middle House Farm

Gordale Scar.

M Ranks
1996

Map 60
Malham YH to Kettlewell YH: part 2

Looking back at Malham Tarn from Monk's Road

Village of Arncliffe

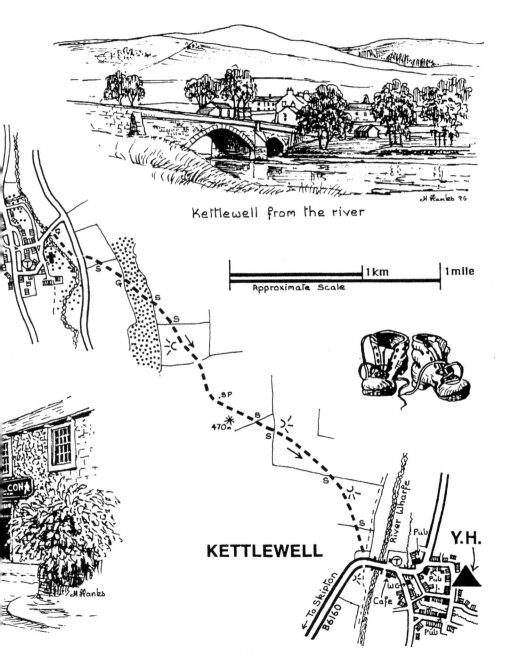

Kettlewell from the river

1 km   1 mile
Approximate Scale

470m

KETTLEWELL

River Wharfe

Pub

Y.H.

To Skipton

B6160

WC

Cafe

Pub

Pub

Map 61
Boggle Hole YH to Wheeldale YH: part 1
see page 159

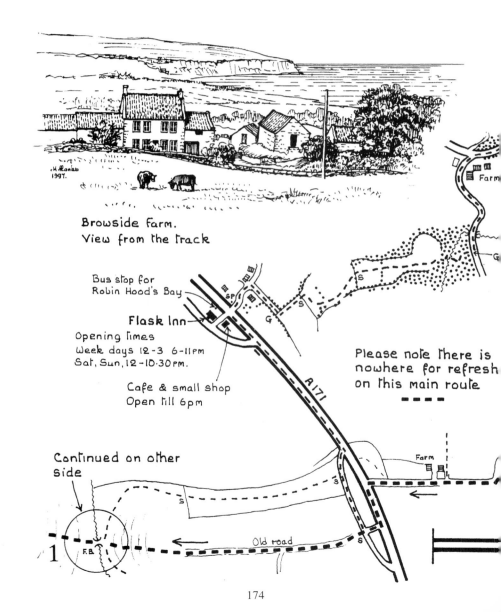

Browside Farm.
View from the track

Bus stop for
Robin Hood's Bay

Flask Inn
Opening times
Week days 12-3 6-11pm
Sat, Sun, 12-10.30pm.

Cafe & small shop
Open till 6pm

Please note there is
nowhere for refresh
on this main route

Continued on other
side

Old road

174

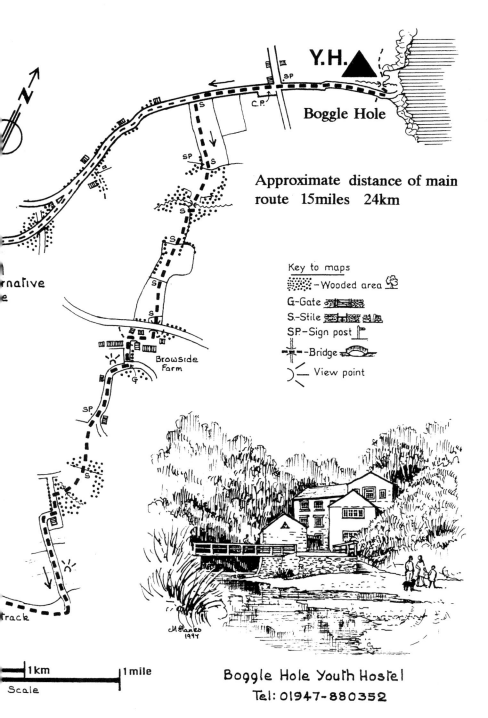

Y.H. ▲

Boggle Hole

Approximate distance of main route 15miles 24km

Key to maps

▒ – Wooded area 🌳
G – Gate
S – Stile
SP – Sign post
– Bridge
View point

Browside Farm

Alternative

Track

1km   1mile

Scale

Boggle Hole Youth Hostel
Tel: 01947-880352

175

It is essential that an O.S. map is used when making this section of this walk as there are few landmarks and the track is poorly defined in places.

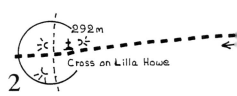

292m

Cross on Lilla Howe

2

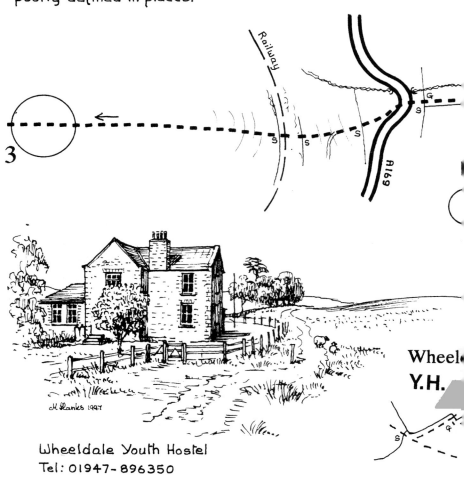

Railway

A169

3

Wheeldale Youth Hostel
Tel: 01947-896350

Wheel...
Y.H.

Designed by M Hanks

Map 62
Boggle Hole YH to Wheeldale YH: part 2

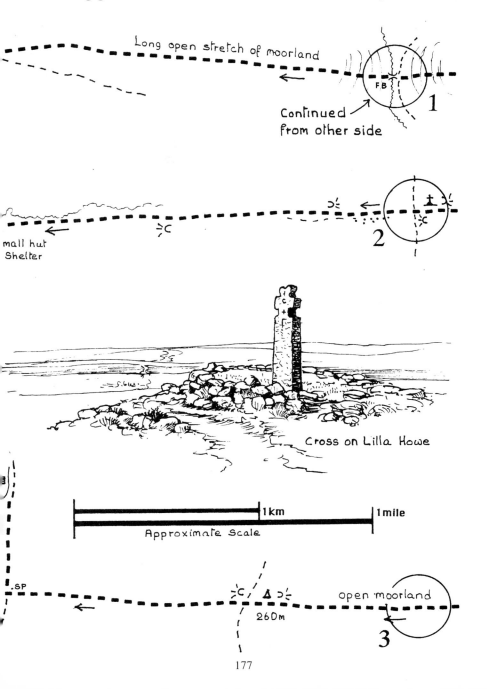

Long open stretch of moorland

Continued
from other side

FB

1

mall hut
Shelter

2

Cross on Lilla Howe

1km   1mile
Approximate Scale

.SP

open moorland

260m

3

Map 63
Scarborough YH to Lockton YH: part 1
see page 159

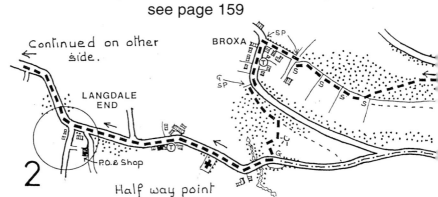

Continued on other side.

LANGDALE END

BROXA

P.O. & Shop

2

Half way point

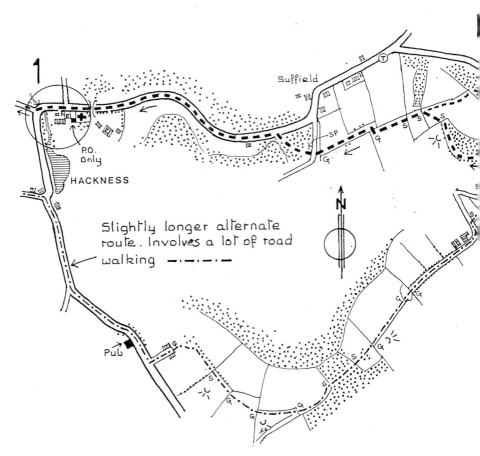

1

Suffield

P.O. Only

HACKNESS

Slightly longer alternate route. Involves a lot of road walking —·—·—·—

N

Pub

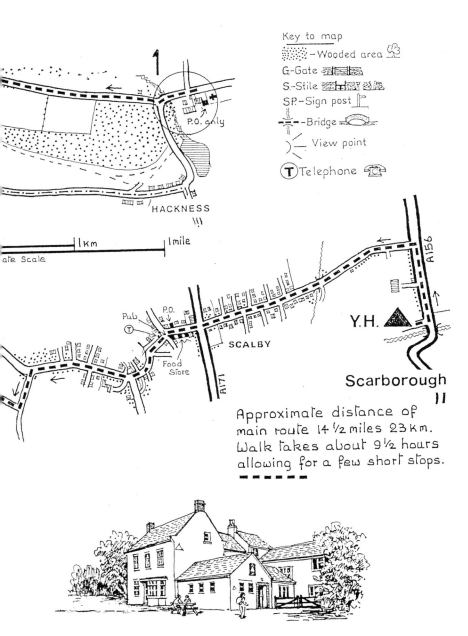

Key to map
- ▓▓▓ – Wooded area
- G – Gate
- S – Stile
- SP – Sign post
- ✝ – Bridge
- ☼ – View point
- (T) Telephone

HACKNESS

1 Km   1 mile

ate Scale

Pub
P.O.
(T)

SCALBY

Food Store

A171

Y.H. ▲

Scarborough

A156

Approximate distance of
main route 14½ miles 23 km.
Walk takes about 9½ hours
allowing for a few short stops.

Scarborough Youth Hostel. Tel 01723-361176

179

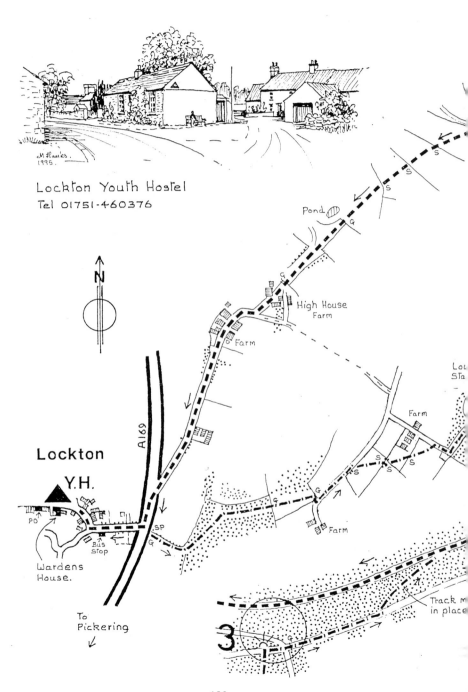

Lockton Youth Hostel
Tel 01751-460376

N

Pond

High House
Farm

Farm

A169

Lockton

Y.H.

PO

Wardens
House.

Bus
Stop

SP

Farm

Farm

Lo...
Sta...

Track m...
in place

3

To
Pickering

Map 63
Scarborough YH to Lockton YH: part 2

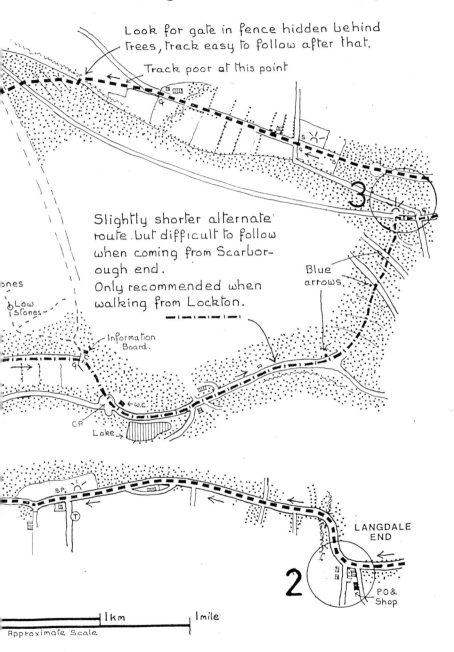

Look for gate in fence hidden behind trees, track easy to follow after that.

Track poor at this point

Slightly shorter alternate route. but difficult to follow when coming from Scarborough end.
Only recommended when walking from Lockton.

Blue arrows

Information Board.

ones

Low Stones

← w.c.

C.P.

Lake →

LANGDALE END

PO & Shop

1km   1mile

Approximate Scale

Wheeldale YH to Lockton YH   8 miles (12.7km)

Map 64 (see pages 184/185 and 186/187)

This path climbs up onto Lockton High Moor before dropping through the Hole of Horcum to Lockton YH. The path heads south from Wheeldale YH to the Blawath Beck before entering the northern edge of Cropton Forest. It passes the ruin of Wardle Green and continues eastwards, dropping down into Newton Dale and crossing the North Yorkshire Moors Railway which is now a preserved line. From here, the route leaves the Forest and heads for the Saltergate Inn on the A169 Pickering to Whitby road.

After refreshments at the inn, the path to Lockton can be chosen from a variety of routes. There is a route across Levisham Moor, with good views over the moors, or you can descend through the Hole of Horcum and follow the Levisham Beck to Levisham, just to the north of Lockton. There is a longer route via the Bride Stones which is also referred to under **Walks around Lockton YH**. This extends the route by a mile (2km).

Cycle Routes around Slaidburn

Map 65 (see page188/189)

This map is useful for its general information and can be used by motorists too. There are three routes: to Bleasdale (35 miles/56km); to Clitheroe (18 miles/28.5km) and to Settle and Clapham (30 miles/48km).

Cycle Routes around Beverley

Map 66 (see page 190/191)

Beverley to Hornsea   34 miles (54km)

Take Long Lane past Dak's Garden Centre over the level crossing to the A1174. At the roundabout turn left on the A1033 Cycle path and then turn left for Wawne and Skerlaugh. Look out for Meaux Abbey just over the Holdnerness Drain.

From Skirlaugh, take the lane to New Ellerby and then join the old railway line to cycle to Hornsea. There is a cafe at the boathouse on Hornsea Mere. Return on the B1244 through Catwick to Leven. Take the A1035 from here through Routh and Tickton to return to Beverley.

Map 67 (see page 192/193)

Beverley to North Newbald   26 miles (41.5km)

Take Long Lane from Beverley and continue south on Park Lane towards Cottingham. On reaching the B1233 go west to Skidby via the restored Skidby Windmill, built in 1821. Take the lane to Little Weighton and continue westwards to South Newbald and then North Newbald where there is a fine Norman Church. From here head for the A1079 past the Northern Shire House Centre and cafe. Beyond the A1079 is the Hudson Way on the old railway line between Beverley and Market Weighton. This takes you directly back to Beverley.

Beverley to Walkington   20 miles (32km)

Take the previous route to Little Weighton. Turn right here for Walkington, continuing on through Bishop Burton and Cherry Burton to reach the Hudson Way, an old rail trail. Join this and turn eastwards (to the right) to return directly to Beverley. There is a short circular extention to the above routes of eight miles (12.8Km), which takes you to the Yorkshire Water Museum near Willerby.

Beverley to North Newbald and North Dalton   34 miles (54km)

Take the North Newbald route above and at the Hudson Way, turn west. Upon reaching the former old Leplingcotes Station (refreshments available), go north to Middleton-on-the-Wold to North Dalton where there is a cafe at the old School. There is a circuitous route back to Beverley taking in a number of small interesting villages and the Beswick Watermill – a restored flour mill with a farm and nature walk.

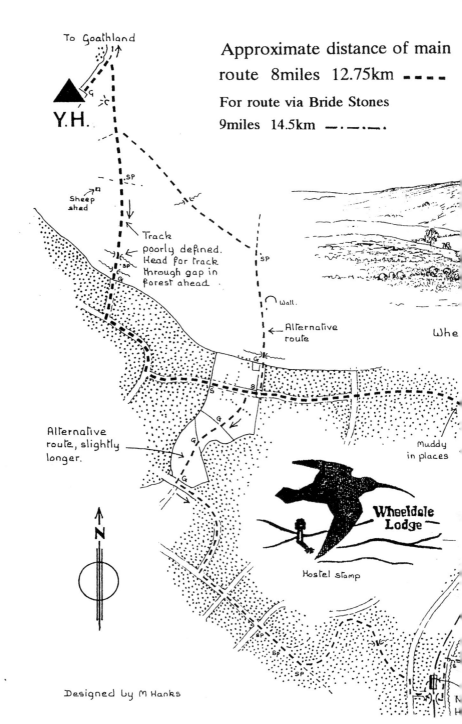

To Goathland

Y.H.

Approximate distance of main route 8miles 12.75km - - - -

For route via Bride Stones 9miles 14.5km —.—.—.

SP

Sheep shed

Track poorly defined. Head for track through gap in forest ahead.

SP

Wall.

Alternative route

Whe

Alternative route, slightly longer.

Muddy in places

N

Wheeldale Lodge

Hostel stamp

Designed by M Hanks

184

Map 64
Wheeldale YH to Lockton YH: part 1
see page 182

Key to maps
- Wooded area
- G-Gate
- S-Stile
- SP-Sign post
- Bridge
-)(View point
- (T) Telephone

Hostel
Tel: 01947·896350

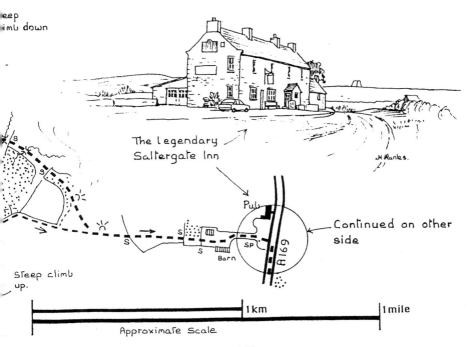

eep
imb down

Steep climb
up.

The legendary
Saltergate Inn

M. Ranks.

Pub

SP

Barn

A169

Continued on other
side

1 km   1 mile

Approximate Scale

185

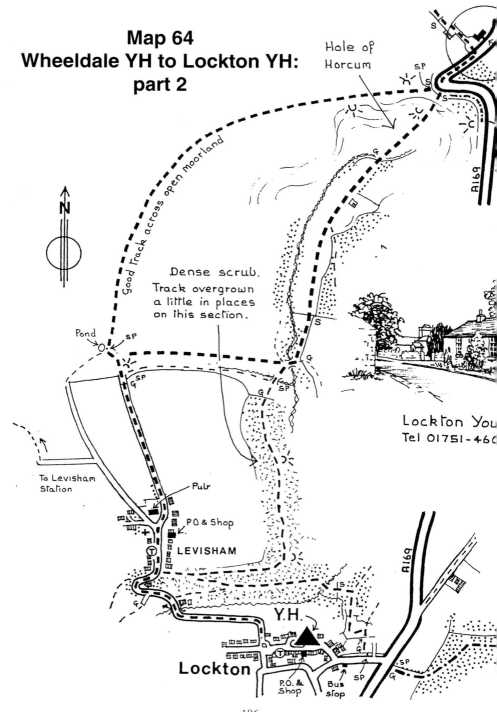

Map 64
Wheeldale YH to Lockton YH:
part 2

Hole of Horcum

Good Track across open moorland

Dense scrub. Track overgrown a little in places on this section.

Pond

To Levisham Station

Pub

PO & Shop

LEVISHAM

Lockton You
Tel 01751-46(

Y.H.

Lockton

P.O. & Shop

Bus stop

A169

186

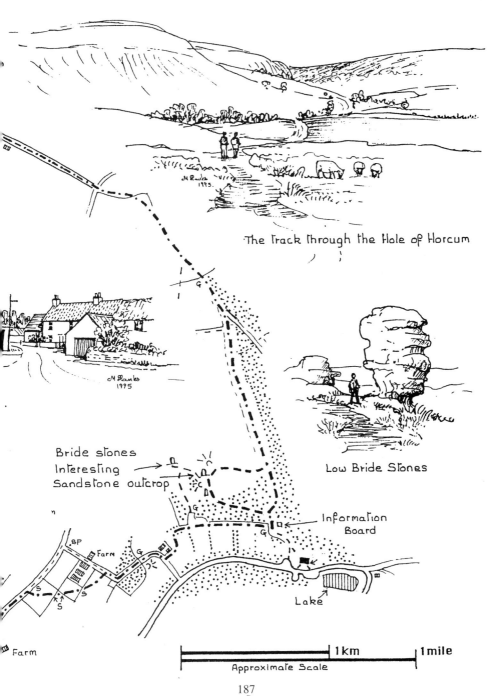

The Track Through the Hole of Horcum

Low Bride Stones

Bride stones
Interesting
Sandstone outcrop

Information
Board

Farm

SP
Farm

Lake

1km   1mile

Approximate Scale

Map 65 Cycle routes around Slaidburn YH

Circular cycle routes
and places of interest
within 13 Miles 20½ Km
of the hostel.

All 3 of these routes take in
unspoilt attractive scenery
with fine views, but involve
a bit of hard climbing.

Clapham

Slaidburn Hostel.
☎:01200-446656

Round Trip
35 miles
56 Km.
- - - - -

To Lancaster

Trough of Bowland

1000 Ft

Chipping.
Attractive village
Good cafe
2 pubs & shop

Pub
Good
Food

Cafe
Bleasdale

To Longridge

Stony
Colleg

Clitheroe
Old market tow
Castle - Muse
Information off
Ribblesdale Poo

N

Trough of Bowland

188

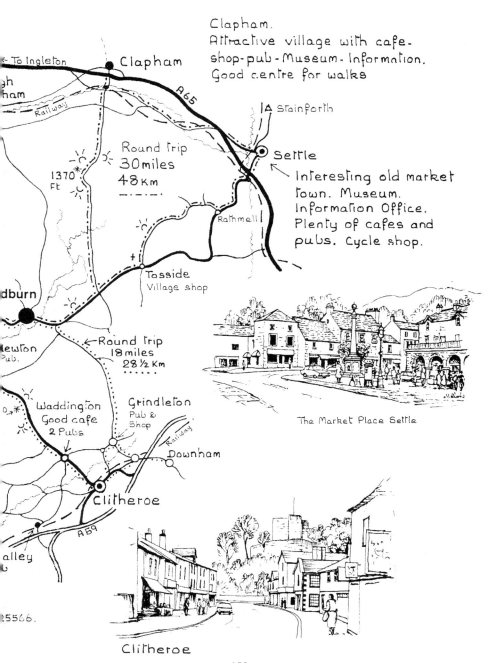

Clapham.
Attractive village with cafe-
shop-pub-Museum. Information.
Good centre for walks

To Ingleton

Clapham

A65

Railway

A Stainforth

Round trip
30 miles
48 Km

1370 Ft

Rathmell

Settle
Interesting old market
town. Museum.
Information Office.
Plenty of cafes and
pubs. Cycle shop.

Tosside
Village shop

dburn

Round trip
18 miles
28½ Km

Newton
Pub.

Waddington
Good cafe
2 Pubs

Grindleton
Pub &
Shop

Railway

Downham

Clitheroe

A59

alley

5566.

The Market Place Settle

Clitheroe

189

Map 66 Cycle routes around Beverley YH: Beverley to Hornsea

see page 183

Beverley Friary Youth Hostel Tel: 01482-881751

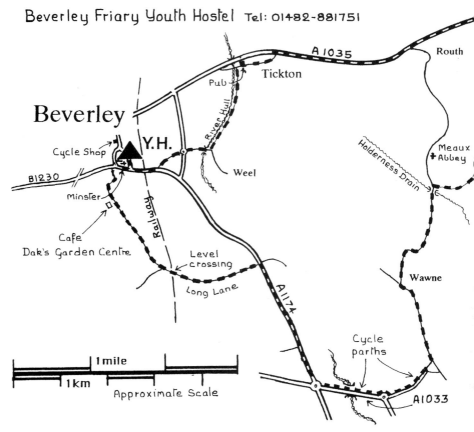

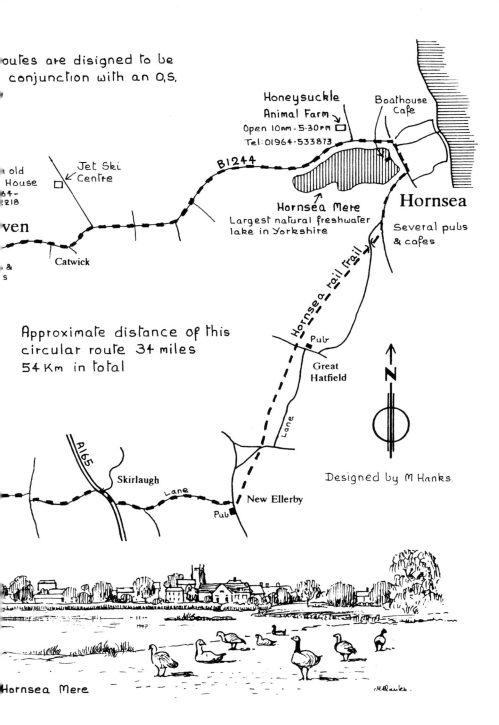

outes are disigned to be
conjunction with an O.S.

Honeysuckle
Animal Farm
Open 10am-5.30pm
Tel: 01964·533873

Boathouse
Cafe

B1244

old
House
64-
218

Jet Ski
Centre

ven

Catwick

&
S

Hornsea Mere
Largest natural freshwater
lake in Yorkshire

Hornsea

Several pubs
& cafes

Hornsea rail trail

Approximate distance of this
circular route 34 miles
54 Km in total

Pub

Great
Hatfield

N

Lane

A165

Skirlaugh

Lane

Pub

New Ellerby

Designed by M Hanks.

Hornsea Mere

M.Hanks.

191

Map 67　Cycle routes around Beverley YH:
Beverley to North Newbald and North Dalton

see page 183

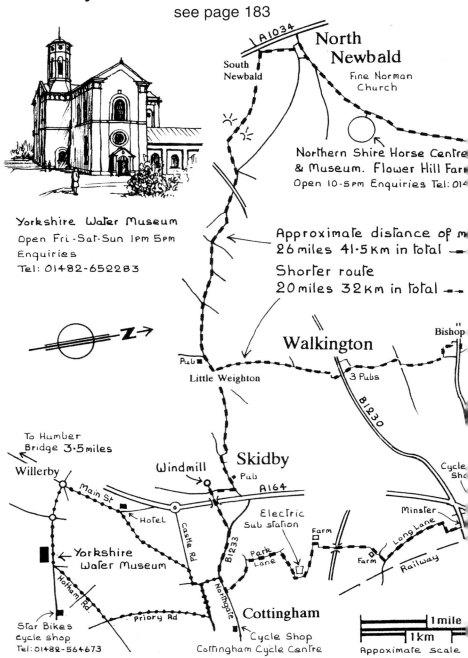

North Newbald

A1034

South Newbald

Fine Norman Church

Northern Shire Horse Centre & Museum. Flower Hill Farm
Open 10-5pm Enquiries Tel: 014

Yorkshire Water Museum
Open Fri-Sat-Sun 1pm 5pm
Enquiries
Tel: 01482-652283

Approximate distance of m
26 miles 41.5Km in total ▬▶

Shorter route
20 miles 32Km in total ▬▶

Walkington

Bishop

Z→

Pub ▪

Little Weighton

3 Pubs

B1230

To Humber
Bridge 3.5 miles

Willerby

Skidby

Windmill

Pub

A164

Cycle Sho

Main St

Hotel

Castle Rd

Electric
Sub station

Farm

Minster

Long Lane

▪ Yorkshire
Water Museum

B1233

Park
Lane

Farm

Railway

Hotham Rd

Northgate

Cottingham

Star Bikes
cycle shop
Tel:01482-564673

Priory Rd

Cycle Shop
Cottingham Cycle Centre

1mile
1km
Appoximate scale

192

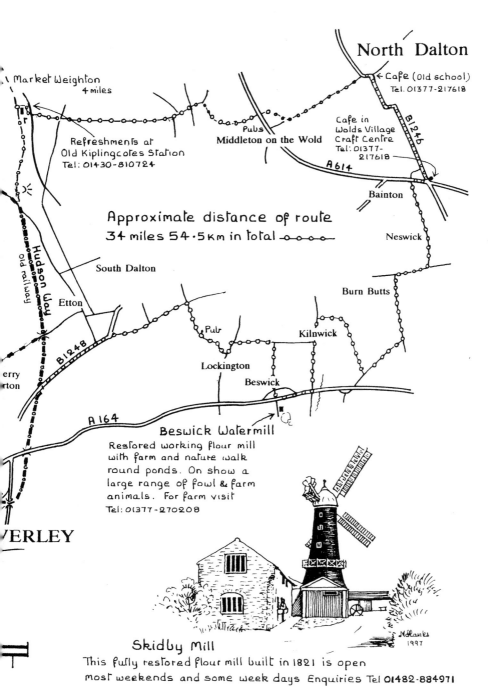

North Dalton

← Café (Old school)
Tel. 01377-217618

Market Weighton
4 miles

Café in
Wolds Village
Craft Centre
Tel: 01377-217618

B1246

Pubs
Middleton on the Wold

Refreshments at
Old Kiplingcotes Station
Tel: 01430-810724

A614

Bainton

Neswick

Approximate distance of route
34 miles 54·5 km in total

South Dalton

Burn Butts

Hudson Way
Old railway

Etton

Pulr

Kilnwick

B1248

Lockington

Beswick

erry
ton

A164

Beswick Watermill

Restored working flour mill
with farm and nature walk
round ponds. On show a
large range of fowl & farm
animals. For farm visit
Tel: 01377-270208

VERLEY

N. Hawkes
1997

Skidby Mill

This fully restored flour mill built in 1821 is open
most weekends and some week days Enquiries Tel 01482-884971

LANDMARK VISITORS GUIDES

* **Practical guides for the independent traveller**

* **Written in the form of touring itineraries**

* **Full colour illustrations and maps**

* **Detailed Landmark FactFile of practical information**

* **Landmark Visitors Guides highlight all the interesting places you will want to see, so ensuring that you make the most of your visit**

1. **Britain**
   Cornwall
   Devon
   Jersey
   Peak District
   Dorset
   Guernsey

   Cotswolds & Shakespeare Country
   Edinburgh
   Lake District
   Scotland
   York & Yorkshire Dales
   Hampshire & Isle of Wight

2. **Europe**
   Bruges
   Provence
   Italian Lakes
   Norway

   Black Forest
   Florence & Tuscany
   Gran Canaria

3. **Other**
   India: Kerala & The South
   Florida – Gulf Coast
   Florida – Atlantic Coast

   Florida Keys
   Orlando & Central Florida

LANDMARK
Publishing Ltd ● ● ●

Waterloo House, 12 Compton, Ashbourne,
Derbyshire DE6 1DA England
Tel: 01335 347349   Fax: 01335 347303

THE YOUTH HOSTELS

Aysgarth Falls YH

Aysgarth, Leyburn,
North Yorkshire DL8 3SR
Tel: 01969 663260 Fax: 01969 663110

Accommodation details:

It has six 3-4 bedded and six 5-8 bedded rooms and access during the day. Facilities include lounge, TV room, games room, self-catering kitchen, showers and dryingroom. Cycle shed. Dinner served at 19.00.
Open: end-January to Easter Friday and Saturday; 1 April to 30 June excluding Sundays; 1 July to 31 August daily; 1 September to 31 October excluding Sundays; November Friday and Saturday; 28 December to 3 January and Bank Holiday Sundays.

Getting there:-

The hostel is 1/2 mile east of Aysgarth on the A684.
By bus: United 26 from Richmond (infrequent), connections from Railway Station Darlington (Tel: 01325 468771). Dales Bus from West Yorkshire (Tel: 01423 566061); Postbus from Northallerton (weekdays).
By rail: Garsdale 16m (25.6km); Northallerton 24m (38.4km); Skipton 28m (44.8km).

Description:

Aysgarth Falls Youth Hostel is a warm and friendly base from which to explore the area. Accommodation is ideal for families and groups and the hostel is situated just a minute's walk from the famous falls. In the evening the illuminated ruins of nearby Bolton Abbey can be seen.

The hostel lies in the heart of Herriot country, and the Herriot Way is an unofficial long distance walk through Swaledale and Wensleydale taking in some of the beautiful scenery made famous by the James Herriot books and TV series. It is also a popular place for cyclists to stay on the Yorkshire Dales Cycleway.

Boggle Hole YH

Boggle Hole, Mill Beck, Fylingthorpe, Whitby, North Yorshire YO22 4UQ
Tel: 01947 880352 Fax: 01947 880987

Accommodation details:

A former corn mill set in a wooded ravine having many of the bedrooms in an adjacent building. Mostly 4-6 bedded rooms plus one 10 and 16 bedded room. Access during the day: lounge, TV, self-catering kitchen, showers, drying room, cycle shed and lockers available from 13.00. Dinner served 19.00.
Open: mid-February to end-October daily and 27 December to 2 January.

Getting there:

By bus: Tees 93A Scarborough-Whitby (passes Whitby & Scarborough Railway Stations), alight Robin Hood's Bay, 1m. (Tel: 01947 602146).
By rail: Whitby (not Sunday, except June-September) 7m (11.2km); Scarborough 15m (24km).

Description:

Boggle Hole Youth Hostel is quite uniquely situated, only yards from the beach. The grounds extend up the valley and are mainly natural woodland with a great variety of wild flowers, bushes and trees sheltering many birds and animals. Children will love playing on the rocky beach outside the youth hostel and this is also an ideal base from which to explore the surrounding area. Boggle Hole lies on the Coast to Coast path and the Cleveland Way which makes it popular with walkers.

Dentdale YH

Cowgill, Dent, Sedbergh,
Cumbria LA10 5RN
Tel/Fax: 015396 25251

Accommodation details:

A former shooting lodge in the upper reaches of Dentdale having one 8, two 10 and one 12 bedded rooms. Access during day: lounge, toilets and washrooms open 12.00. Other facilities include: lounge with open fire, self-catering kitchen, showers, drying room and cycle shed. Dinner served 19.00.

Open: 31 January to end-February Friday and Saturday; March excluding Wednesday/Thursday; 1 April to end-August excluding Thursday; 1 September to end-October excluding Wednesday/Thursday; 1 November to 21 December Friday and Saturday; 27 December to 3 January.

Getting there:

Take Dentdale road north-east of Whernside, 2m (3.2km) from junction with Hawes-Ingleton road 5m (8km) east of Dent. Width restriction 7.5ft at Cowgill, large vehicles approach via Newby Head.

By bus: Harrington Railway Station from Garsdale Railway Station(Tel: 01969 650682); United 26 from Richmond (infrequent) (connections from Darlington) (Tel: 01325 468771), alight at Hawes, thence 8m (12.8km).

By rail: Dent 2m (3.2km); Giggleswick 17.5m (28.8km).

Description:

Deeside House has been a youth hostel since 1944. It is situated in a beautiful location high up Dentdale and convenient for those wishing to walk the 'Three Peaks' of Whernside, Ingleborough and Pen-y-ghent or the Dales Way, running from Ilkley to Windermere. The hostel is an ideal place for cyclists to stay on the Yorkshire Dales Cycleway.

One of the best introductions to the area is "Walking the Dales" by Mike Harding. Dent village is situated five miles down the Dentdale valley. This quaint village, once famous for its knitting, comprises old houses grouped around the narrow cobbled streets with cafes, shops, a post office and pubs.

The dale is rich in caves and waterfalls and is a Geologist's delight with examples of limestone beds, fossils and Dent marble. White Scar caves — site of England's biggest cave — are only 8 miles away and are open to the public with guided tours all year round.

Along the fells of the upper Dentdale valley runs the Settle to Carlisle railway, the country's finest and highest scenic main line. During the summer, special steam hauled charters run several times a month, crossing viaducts and sweeping through tunnels. Only a few minutes walk from the Youth Hostel is the impressive Arten Gill viaduct — the piers of which plunge 50ft into the ground in search of solid rock.

Earby YH

Katherine Bruce-Glasier Memorial Hostel, Glen Cottage, 9-11 Birch Hall Lane, Earby, Colne, Lancs BB8 6JX
Tel: 01282 842349

Accommodation details:

This hostel has one 2, two 6 and one 8 bedded rooms. There is access during the day to toilet, drying room, conservatory, shower and garden. Other facilities include: lounge, shower, self-catering kitchen, and cycle shed. Self-catering only, no shop.
Open: Easter to end-September daily (excluding Tuesday); 1 October to Easter on Rent-a-Hostel scheme.

Getting there:

The hostel is 300yd beyond the Red Lion public house.
By bus: Various services from Burnley, Skipton (passing close to Colne & Skipton Railway Station), alight Earby, 1/2m (Tel: 01257 241693). National Express coach from London to Skipton.
By rail: Colne 5m (8km); Skipton 8m (12.8km). Settle to Carlisle line at Skipton.

Description:

Glen Cottage is a small cosy hostel with picturesque garden and waterfalls close to the Pennine Way. Recently extensively refurbished, it now provides excellent self-catering accommodation for all types of visitors. There is a well equipped kitchen and dining room, cosy common room and good washing facilities with three showers. There is also a drying room and small shop, and a cycle shed.

Ellingstring YH

Lilac Cottage, Ellingstring, Masham, Nr Ripon, North Yorkshire HG4 4PW
Tel: 01677 460216 (Warden's phone)
Or book via: Mrs A C Wright, Hollybreen, Ellingstring, Ripon, North Yorkshire HG4 4PW

Accommodation details:

This hostel has one 4 and two 8 bedded rooms. There is access during the day to the cycle shed. Other facilities include: common room, very well equipped self-catering kitchen including microwave oven, shower and solid fuel central heating. Self-catering only.
Open: 1 November to Easter on Rent-a-Hostel scheme; Easter to end-June excluding Wednesday/Thursday; 1 July to 31 August daily; 1 September to end-October excluding Wednesday/Thursday.

Getting there:

By bus: United 159 (infrequent) from Ripon to within 1m (Tel: 01325 468771); otherwise Postbus from Ripon (Tel: 01532 447470) or Dales Bus (Tel: 01423 566061).
By rail: Thirsk 16m (25.6km); Northallerton 17m (27.2km).

Description:

Get away from it all by staying in this attractive stone built cottage in a small hamlet in the Yorkshire Dales. Perfectly placed for walking and cycling. Close by is the old market town of Masham with its ancient church of St Marys. There are numerous craft shops at the rear of the Kings Head pub in the Market Place. A recent development has been the Black Sheep Brewery by Paul Theakston. It has an interesting visitor centre and bistro, plus of course, wonderful beer!

Grinton Lodge YH

Grinton, Richmond, North Yorkshire DL11 6HS
Tel: 01748 884206 Fax: 01748 884 876

Accommodation details:

A former shooting lodge high on Harkerside Moor. It has one 2, three 4, two 6 and five 8 bedded rooms. Access during the day: self-catering kitchen, TV lounge, toilets, drying room and laundry. Other facilities include: games room, showers, quiet room, cycle shed, bike hire and grounds. Dinner served 19.00.
Open: 1 January to Easter excluding Sunday/Monday; Easter to end-August daily; 1 September to end-October excluding Sunday; 27 December to 3 January.

Getting there:

Due south from Grinton for 3/4 mile on Reeth-Leyburn Road.
By bus: United 30 Richmond-Keld (infrequent) (connections from Darlington Railway Station), alight Grinton, 3/4m (Tel: 01325 468771); Dales Bus from West Yorkshire (Tel: 01423 566061).
By rail: Kirkby Stephen 24m (38.4km); Darlington 25m (40km).

Description:

Grinton Lodge, ten miles from Richmond, stands high on the heather clad slopes overlooking Swaledale and Arkengarthdale. Families are most welcome at Grinton Lodge and are well provided for by the amenities and the catering service. Swaledale is an excellent area for all sorts of activities from bird-watching to caving. There are many walks in the area, from pleasant strolls to challenge routes and, the historic market town of Richmond is only ten miles away with its castle, three museums and Georgian Theatre Royal.

Hawes YH

Lancaster Terrace, Hawes, North Yorkshire DL8 3LQ
Tel: 01969 667368 Fax: 01969 667723

Accommodation details:

A modern building overlooking the village of Hawes and Wensleydale beyond. It has two 2, three 3, two 4, one 5 and four 8 bedded rooms. Access during the day: porch, drying room and cycle shed. Other facilities include: lounge, TV room, games room, self-catering kitchen, showers, drying room, cycle shed and laundry facilities. Dinner served 19.00.
Open: 1 March to Easter excluding Wednesday/Thursday; Easter to 30 June excluding Sunday; 1 July to 31 August daily; 1 September to 21 December excluding Monday/Tuesday; 23 to 27 December. Open Bank Holiday Sundays.

Getting there:

West of Hawes on the Ingleton Road.
By bus: BR Harrington from BR Garsdale (Tel: 01969 650682); United 26 from Richmond (infrequent with connections from BR Darlington, Tel: 01325 468771).
By rail: Garsdale 6m (9.6km).

Description:

Hawes Youth Hostel in the centre of the Yorkshire Dales National Park is ideally situated for walking, cycling and visiting local places of interest including Askrigg, Castle Bolton, Jervaulx Abbey, Middleham Castle, Settle-Carlisle Railway, Hardraw Force and Semerwater.

Haworth YH

Longlands Hall, Longlands Drive, Lees Lane, Haworth, Keighley, West Yorkshire BD22 8RT
Tel: 01535 642234 Fax: 01535 643023

Accommodation details:

Victorian mansion set in its own grounds overlooking the famous Brontë village. A few 2-6 bedded rooms, mostly 8-14 bedded rooms. Access during the day: lounge, self-catering kitchen, showers, drying room, cycle shed, laundry facilities and grounds. Dinner served 18.30.
Open: 31 January to Easter excluding Sunday; Easter to 30 September daily; 1 October to 21 December excluding Sunday; 27 December to 3 January.

Getting there:

By bus: Keighley & District 500, 663/664/665, 720, CalderLine 500, Calder Coaches M2-4 from Keighley (pass close Keighley Railway Station) (Tel: 0113 2457676).
By rail: Keighley 4m (6.4km); Haworth (Worth Valley Railway) 0.5m.

Description:

Longlands Hall was formerly the home of a local mill owner. It is set in its own grounds and overlooks the famous Bronte village. Inside the building, the sweeping staircase, ornate painted glass, richly carved oak and strange plaster friezes hint at the building's opulent past.

As a Youth Hostel it now provides a welcome resting place for walkers and international tourists. The hostel is also very popular with groups of children. The staff specialise in home cooking and like to give very a warm welcome.

Helmsley YH

Carlton Lane, Helmsley, North Yorkshire YO6 5HB
Tel/Fax: 01439 770433

Accommodation details:

Helmsley Youth Hostel has two 4, three 6-8 and one 10 bedded rooms. Access during the day: cycle shed, drying room and porch. Other facilities include: lounge, self-catering kitchen, showers, laundry facilities and grounds. Dinner served 19.00.
Open: 1-6 January; 7 January to Easter, Monday to Thursday, Rent-a-Hostel Friday/Saturday; Easter to mid-July daily excluding Sunday; mid-July to 30 August daily; 31 August to 1 November daily excluding Sunday; 2 November to 31 December Rent-a-Hostel scheme. Open Bank Holiday Sundays.

Getting there:

The hostel is 1/4m east of Helmsley market place at junction of Carlton Road and Carlton Lane (just off A170).
By bus: Stevensons 57/58 from York Railway Station (Tel: 01347 838990); Scarborough & District 128 from Scarborough (passes close Scarborough Railway Station) (Tel: 01723 375463).
By rail: Thirsk 15m (24km); Malton 16m (25.6km); York 24m (38.4km).

Description:

Helmsley is a modern and comfortable hostel in the centre of this small country town. It is an excellent base for activities in particular walking and cycling. It has its own ruined castle which was once an impressive stronghold, and is now open to the public.

Ingleton YH

Greta Tower, Sammy Lane, Ingleton, Carnforth, Lancashire LA6 3EG
Tel: 015242 41444 Fax: 015242 41854

Accommodation details:

An old stone house in its own gardens close to the centre of the village. It has four 4, six 6 and one 14 bedded rooms. Access during the day: self-catering kitchen, drying room, lounge and toilets. Other facilities include: showers, cycle shed and grounds. Dinner served 19.00.

Open: 3-31 January Friday/Saturday/Sunday; 1 February to Easter excluding Sunday/Monday; Easter to 30 June excluding Sunday; 1 July to 31 August daily; 1-30 September excluding Sunday; 1 October to 2 November excluding Sunday/Monday; 23 December to 3 January. Open Bank Holidays.

Getting there:

From High Street take the lane between Barclays Bank and the carpet shop down to the park.
By bus: Stagecoach Ribble X80, 80/1 from Lancaster (passes close Lancaster & Bentham Railway Stations) (Tel: 01257 241693).
By rail: Bentham 3m (4.8km); Clapham 4m (6.4km).

Description:

Ingleton Youth Hostel is situated in its own mature gardens in the heart of Ingleton village on the edge of the Yorkshire Dales National Park. The hostel's location is ideal for access to the Dales, The Lake District, Trough of Bowland and shores of Morecambe Bay. Activities available from the hostel include cycling, walking, climbing, caving and abseiling. The wardens can arrange for a qualified local instructor to help organise your activities. The Yorkshire Dales Cycleway is a circular route of approximately 215km through the best of the Dales scenery. Skipton with its castle and church dating back to the 14th century and, the famous Settle-Carlisle railway runs close by, passing over the Ribblehead Viaduct.

Keld YH

Keld Lodge, Upper Swaledale, Richmond, North Yorkshire DL11 6LL
Tel: 01748 886259 Fax: 01748 886013

Accommodation details:

This former shooting lodge is high in upper Swaledale and has mostly 4 and 6 bedded plus one 10 bedded room. Access during the day: limited to porch only. Other facilities include: lounge, TV, self-catering kitchen, showers, drying room and cycle shed. Dinner served 19.00.

Open: 3 January to Easter excluding Tuesday/Wednesday/Thursday; Easter to 30 June excluding Monday; 1 July to 31 August daily; 1 September to 31 October excluding Monday/Tuesday; 1-30 November excluding Tuesday/Wednesday/Thursday; 27 December to 3 January.

Getting there:

Situated west of Keld village on B6270 Reeth to Kirkby Stephen Road.
By bus: United 30 from Richmond (infrequent with connections from Darlington Railway Station, Tel: 01325 468771); Dales Bus (Tel: 01423 566061).
By rail: Kirkby Stephen 11m (17.6km).

Description:

Keld Youth Hostel is a former shooting lodge, set high in upper Swaledale, it is now a compact cosy hostel with mostly small bedrooms and a lounge with open fire. The hostel is set amongst meadows and waterfalls.

Kettlewell YH

Whernside House, Kettlewell, Skipton, North Yorkshire BD23 5QU
Tel: 01756 760232 Fax: 01756 760402

Accommodation details:

An old stone house in the centre of the village with three 2, two 4, five 6 and two 7 bedded rooms. Access during the day: drying room, showers, self-catering kitchen, common room and toilets. Other facilities include: lounge/dining room, TV, cycle shed, lockers and grounds. Adjoining the hostel, is a self-contained 10 bedded unit, with it's own facilities, ideal for families and small groups. Dinner served 19.00.
Open: 31 January to Easter excluding Wednesday/Thursday; Easter to 30 September daily; 1 October to 20 December excluding Wednesday/Thursday; 27 December to 3 January.

Getting there:

By bus: Pride of the Dales 72 from Skipton Railway Station, alight Grassington 6m (9.6km) (Tel: 01756 753123). Local coach company Hargreaves (based near Grassington Tel: 01756 752567)
By rail: Skipton 16m (25.6km). (Tel: 01756 792543).

Description:

Kettlewell Youth Hostel is situated in a picturesque village in the heart of the Yorkshire Dales National Park. It is set amidst dramatic limestone scenery in Upper Wharfedale and makes a good residential base. Activities available with local organisations include caving, gorge scrambling, rock climbing, abseiling, mountain-biking, orienteering, raft building, pony-trekking and walking.

Kirkby Stephen YH

Fletcher Hill, Market Street, Kirkby Stephen, Cumbria CA17 4QQ
Tel/Fax: 017683 71793

Accommodation details:

A former chapel on the main street of this historic market town. It has one 2, two 4, three 6 and two 8 bedded rooms. Access during the day: cycle shed. Other facilities include: lounge, self-catering kitchen, showers, drying room, luggage store and laundry facilities. Dinner served 19.00.
Open: 14 February to Easter Friday/Saturday only; Easter to 1 May excluding Tuesday/Wednesday; 2 May to 31 August excluding Tuesday; 1 September to 1 November excluding Tuesday/Wednesday; 2 November to 20 December Friday/Saturday only.

Getting there:

The hostel is in the centre of the town on main street A685. 12m (19.2km) from M6 junction 38 or 2m (3.2km) from A66 at Brough.
By bus: OK X74 Darlington-Carlisle (Tel: 01388 604581); Primrose Coaches Newcastle-upon-Tyne-Blackpool (passes Kirkby Stephen Railway Station) (Tel: 0191 413 2257).
By rail: Kirkby Stephen 1.5m (2.4km).

Description:

Kirkby Stephen hostel is an attractive, imaginative conversion of an old Methodist chapel on the main street. There are three nature reserves near to the hostel and several places of interest to visit including Brough and Pendragon Castles, Appleby (famous for Appleby New Fair which attracts horse dealers, gypsies and visitors from all over the country), The Bowes Museum and Carlisle-Settle Railway. It has excellent access to both the Yorkshire Dales and Lake District for walkers and several cycling routes converge on Kirkby Stephen.

Linton YH

The Old Rectory, Linton-in-Craven, Skipton, North Yorkshire BD23 5HH
Tel/Fax: 01756 752400

Accommodation details:

A 17th century rectory built of mellow stone a mile from the busier village of Grassington. It has two 4, two 6, one 8 and one 10 bedded rooms. Access during the day: entrance porch and toilet. Other facilities include: lounge, garden with large lawn, self-catering kitchen, showers, drying room and cycle store. Dinner served 19.00.

Open: 1-5 January Rent-a-Hostel scheme; 6 January to 2 March open Monday to Thursday, Rent-a-Hostel Friday/Saturday; Easter to 30 September excluding Sunday; 1-31 October excluding Sunday/Monday; 1 November to 20 December open Monday to Thursday, Rent-a-Hostel Friday/Saturday; 21 December to 4 January. Open Bank Holiday Sundays.

Getting there:

The hostel is adjacent to village green (east side of packhorse bridge over river).
By bus: Pride of the Dales 72 from Skipton Railway Station, alight Linton (Tel: 01535 603284).
By rail: Skipton 8m (12.8km) Tel: (01532 448133).

Description:

This hostel dates from the 17th century and stands in its own grounds beside the village green. The area provides opportunities for a wide range of outdoor activities including walking, climbing, cycling and canoeing. Places of interest to visit in the area include Grassington, Bolton Abbey, Skipton, Hubberholme, Fountains Abbey and Studley Royal.

Lockton YH

The Old School, Lockton, Pickering, North Yorkshire YO18 7PY
Tel: 01751 460376

Accommodation details:

Formerly the village school in a rural hamlet just off the main Pickering-Whitby road. It has one 6, one 8 and one 12 bedded room. Access during the day: toilets. Other facilities include: self-catering kitchen, outside toilet and shower, drying room, cycle shed and car park. No shop. Self-catering only.
Open: 1 January to Easter Rent-a-Hostel scheme; Easter to 27 September excluding Sunday; end-September to Spring Rent-a-Hostel scheme. Open Bank Holiday Sundays.

Getting there:

By bus: Yorkshire Coastliner 840 Whitby-Malton (passes close Whitby & Malton Railway Stations) (Tel: 01653 692556).
By rail: Malton 14m (22.4km); Levisham (North York Moors Railway and connecting with at Grosmont Railway Station) 2m (3.2km).

Description:

This small hostel offers simple self-catering facilities. Lockton has no resident warden or shop, and the toilets and shower are in an external block. The hostel does have a cosy common room and full central heating, and a drying room. Lockton is a peaceful haven for walkers and cyclists, with lovely moorland and forest walks nearby. Goathland and Pickering are both just five miles away, and a ride on the North York Moors Steam Railway which passes through some glorious countryside is not to be missed!

Malham YH

Malham, Skipton, North Yorkshire BD23 4DE
Tel: 01729 830321 Fax: 01729 830551

Accommodation details:

A recently refurbished hostel and annexe with an attractive garden for children to play in. It has one 2, four 4, one 5 and nine 6-8 bedded rooms. Access during the day: toilets, drying room, cycle store, TV lounge and luggage drop area. Other facilities include: lounge, self-catering kitchen, showers, lockers, laundry, classroom and grounds. Dinner served 19.00.
Open: 1 January to 20 December; 21-26 December Rent-a-Hostel scheme (30 beds); 27 December to 3 January.

Getting there:

By bus: Pennine 210 from Skipton (passes close to Skipton Railway Station) (Tel: 01756 749215); Dales Bus (Tel: 01423 566061).
By rail: Skipton 13m (20.8km).

Description:

Malham Youth Hostel is superbly located near to the centre of the village and has lots of small bedrooms making it ideal for families as well as walkers exploring the Yorkshire Dales.
   The hostel is set in extensive grounds, and has a drying room, shop, TV lounge and self catering kitchen, while for those who don't want to cook, there is a full catering service available. There is ample parking at the hostel. Littondale, to the north of Malham, is the location for ITV's "Emmerdale".

Mankinholes YH

Mankinholes, Todmorden, Lancashire OL14 6HR
Tel/Fax: 01706 812340

Accommodation details:

This hostel has five 8 bedded rooms. Access during the day: from 13.00 toilet, self-catering kitchen, lounge and drying room. Other facilities include: showers, cycle shed, luggage store, laundry facilities and grounds. Dinner served 19.00.
Open: 31 January to Easter only Friday/Saturday; Easter to end-August excluding Sunday; 1 September to 31 October excluding Sunday/Monday; 1-30 November only Friday/Saturday. Open Bank Holiday Sundays.

Description:

Mankinholes is a small friendly hostel high in this South Pennines hamlet close to the Pennine Way. The youth hostel is a late 17th century grade II listed building, and was once the local manor house. Accommodation is in eight-bedded rooms. An excellent meals service is available and there is also a self-catering kitchen, shop, cycle shed and drying room. There is plenty of parking for cars in the carpark at the front of the building.

Getting there:

Follow road to Lumbutts, hostel is 1/4m east of Top Brink public house.
By bus: Yorkshire Rider T6 from Todmorden (passes close to Todmorden Railway Station) (Tel: 0113 245 7676).
By rail: Todmorden 2m (3.2km).

Osmotherley YH

Cote Ghyll Osmotherley, Northallerton, North Yorkshire DL6 3AH
Tel: 01609 883575 Fax: 01609 883715

Accommodation details:

A former mill, modern and spacious inside having a few 2-4 bedded rooms but mostly 6-10 bedded rooms. Access during day: toilets, shelter and drying room. Other facilities include: lounge/reception, TV room, self-catering kitchen, showers, dining/games room, cycle shed, laundry and grounds. Dinner served 19.00.
Open: 31 January to early-September; 7 September to early November excluding Sunday/Monday.

Getting there:

Go through village, down private drive past caravan/camping site.
By bus: Tees 90/A Middlesbrough-Northallerton (passes close to Northallerton Railway Station), alight Osmotherley 3/4m. (Tel: 01642 210131).
By rail: Northallerton 8m (12.8km).

Description:

Osmotherley Youth Hostel offers excellent facilities for the visitor to the North Yorkshire Moors. Places to visit are Rievaulx Abbey, Mount Grace Priory, Lightwater Valley Theme Park, North Yorkshire Moors Steam Railway and Beamish Open Air Museum. The hostel lies on the Coast to Coast path.

Scarborough YH

The White House, Burniston Road, Scarborough, North Yorkshire YO13 0DA
Tel: 01723 361176 Fax: 01723 500054

Accommodation details:

A former riverside mill on the edge of this popular seaside resort. It has five 6, one 8, one 12 and one 14 bedded rooms. Access during the day: entrance hall, drying room and toilet. Other facilities include: lounge, self-catering kitchen, showers and cycle shed. Dinner served at 19.00.
Open: 31 January to Easter only Friday/Saturday; Easter to end-July excluding Sunday; end-July to beginning-September daily; beginning-September to mid-December excluding Sunday/Monday; 24-27 December.

Getting there:

From Scarborough follow signs to North Bay Attractions, then A165 to Whitby. Hostel is 2m (3.2km) north of town centre.
By bus: frequent from surrounding areas (Tel: 01723 375463).
By rail: Scarborough 2m (3.2km).

Description:

This hostel is only ten minutes walk from a quiet sandy beach, and is set in an attractive valley on the banks of Scalby Beck. Scarborough is an ideal base for families wanting to combine outstanding countryside with the best of seaside holiday. Places of interest to visit are Whitby, Robin Hood's Bay, Goathland (Heartbeat Country) and Pickering.

Slaidburn YH

King's House, Slaidburn, Clitheroe, Lancashire BB7 3ER
Tel: 01200 446656

Accommodation details:

In the centre of the village this is a former 17th century inn having one 3, one 4, one 5 and one 10 bedded room. There is also a 14 bedded annexe available from May to September. Access during the day: drying room. Other facilities include: lounge, dining room, self-catering kitchen, showers, central heating and cycle shed. Small shop. Self-catering only.
Open: end-October to Easter Rent-a-Hostel

scheme; Easter week daily; April Friday/Saturday; beginning May to end-September daily; end-September to end-October Friday/Saturday.

Getting there:

By bus: Hynburn 110/1 from Clitheroe (calls at Clitheroe Railway Station) (Tel: 01257 241693).
By rail: Clitheroe 8m (12.8km).

Description:

The village of Slaidburn is charming and secluded, off the main tourist routes on the edge of the Forest of Bowland, a little known Area of Outstanding Natural Beauty consisting mainly of lonely moorland and fells.

Once the Black Bull Inn, the youth hostel now offers basic accommodation for walkers and cyclists. There is limited parking for cars at the hostel.

Stainforth YH

'Taitlands', Stainforth, Settle, North Yorkshire BD24 9PA
Tel: 01729 823577 Fax: 01729 825404

Accommodation details:

A listed Georgian country house in wooded gardens, within a few minutes walk of the village. The rooms are mostly 5-12 bedded. Other facilities include: lounge, classroom, self-catering kitchen, showers, drying room, cycle shed and showers. Dinner served at 19.00.
Open: mid-February to Easter Friday/Saturday; Easter to end-April excluding Sunday; 1 May to end-August daily; mid-September to end-October excluding Sunday; November Friday/Saturday.

Getting there:

2m (3.2km) north of Settle. 1/4m south of village on main B6479 Settle-Horton-in-Ribblesdale Road.

Good taxi service (Tel: 01729 822219).
By rail: Settle 2.5m (4km); Giggleswick 3m (4.8km).

Description:

Stainforth Youth Hostel is a listed Georgian country house situated within the Yorkshire Dales National Park, just a few minutes walk from the village and packhorse bridge across the River Ribble. Many of the original period features have been retained, including a marble fireplace and plasterwork ceilings. Facilities include parking, a cycle shed and drying room and shop. The hostel offers a full catering service, and there is a self-catering kitchen.

Thixendale YH

The Village Hall, Thixendale, Malton, North Yorkshire Y)17 9TG
Tel: 01377 288238

Accommodation details:

Formerly the village school, this tiny hostel offers limited facilities. There is one 8 and one 10 bedded room. Facilities include: common/dining room and self catering kitchen. The toilets are outside and there are no showers. Self-catering only.
Open: Easter week; April to Spring Bank Holiday Friday/Saturday; Spring Bank Holiday to end-September excluding Tuesday.

Getting there:

Take the Beverley Road left out of Malton, then right on mini roundabout signposted to Birdsall and Langton. Follow road through Birdsall up the hill, left at the cross roads, signed to Thixendale.
By bus: E Yorkshire 135 from Driffield (infrequent and passes close to Driffield Railway Station), alight Fridaythorpe, 3m (4.8km) (Tel: 01723 375463).
By rail: Malton 10m (16km) (via Birdsall).

Wheeldale YH

Wheeldale Lodge, Goathland, Whitby, North Yorkshire YO22 5AP
Tel: 01947 896350

Accommodation details:

A former shooting lodge surrounded by heather moorland having one 4, 6, 8 and 14 bedded room. Access during the day: cycle shed. Other facilities include: common room, self-catering kitchen, shop, drying room, cycle shed and garden. Bring torch. Self-catering only.
Open: Easter to end-June excluding Wednesday/Thursday; 1 July to end-August excluding Wednesday; 1 September to beginning-October excluding Wednesday/Thursday.

Getting there:

From Goathland take Egton Bridge Road for 1/2m and then turn left on Hunt House road. Continue past the farm on dirt track for 1/4m. Park cars above Hunt House in layby by turning circle and continue on foot.
By bus: Yorkshire Coastliner 840/842 Leeds-York-Malton-Whitby (passes close to Malton and Whitby Railway Stations), alight near Goathland, 2m (3.2km) (Tel: 01653 692556).
By rail: Grosmont (not Sunday, except June-September) 6m (9.6km); Goathland (North York Moors Railway via Grosmont Station) 3m (4.8km).

Description:

Wheeldale Youth Hostel nestles in a small valley close to a stream. It is an excellent alternative high-level route stop for those doing the coast to coast path between Blakley Ridge (Lion Inn) and Robin Hood's Bay (Boggle Hole Youth Hostel).

A haven for walkers, cyclists and nature lovers. Lovely garden surrounded by open moorland. The spring daffodils are well worth seeing and purple heather in September. A friendly oasis in peaceful moorland countryside.

Whitby YH

East Cliff, Whitby, North Yorkshire YO22 4JT
Tel/Fax: 01947 602878

Accommodation details:

Converted from a stable range, the accommodation is basic, with panoramic views of the harbour and coastline. Mostly 10 bedded plus one 6, 8 and 20 bedded room. Access during the day: cycle shed. Other facilities include: lounge, self-catering kitchen, showers, drying room, lockers and garden. Dinner served 19.00.
Open: 1-2 January; end-January to Easter Friday/Saturday; Easter to mid-May excluding Sunday; mid-May to beginning-September daily; beginning-September to end-October excluding Sunday; 1 November to mid-December Friday/Saturday; 31 December to 3 January.

Getting there:

Follow signs to abbey up Green Lane (by road) or up 199 steps.
By bus: frequent from surrounding areas (Tel: 01947 602146).
By rail: Whitby (not Sunday, except June-September) 1/2m.

Description:

Whitby Youth Hostel is situated in a dramatic position, overlooking this fascinating holiday town. Whitby is still an active fishing port of picturesque, sloping cobbled streets, fishermen's cottages, yards and passages. 199 steps lead up to the Abbey from the harbour and Captain Cook, England's greatest navigator, learned his trade in Whitby and a fascinating heritage trail traces his life. There are three miles of sands between Whitby and Sandsend, and the cliff walks in either direction form part of the Cleveland Way National Trail.

FREE OVERNIGHT VOUCHER

Cut out this voucher and present it at the Youth Hostel you are visiting. It will be redeemed for a free overnight stay up to a maximum value of £10.

Free Overnight Voucher
(Value up to £10) Yorkshire Dales & Moors Book

yha

Conditions of use:

1. This voucher can be used at any England & Wales Youth Hostel. It is not redeemable in other countries.
2. It is not redeemable for cash and change cannot be given.
3. Valid only for the item shown and not exchangeable for other YHA services.
4. Valid for part payment (ie. the overnight price) at a bed & breakfast hostel or a family bunkroom.
5. Original voucher will be accepted, no photocopies.

Hostel Stamp

Name ....

Address ....

....

....

Date of Stay:

For Hostel Use: Redeemed Value: £

Hostel Visited: